Ireland's Hidden Diaspora:

The 'abortion trail' and the making of a London-Irish underground, 1980-2000

Ann Rossiter, a long-standing Irish feminist who has been involved in IWASG and Iasc for many years, is from Bruree, Co. Limerick and has lived in London for nearly half a century. She has also been an activist in feminist groups concerned with women and the Irish National Question, such as Women and Ireland and the London Armagh Group. The latter was set up to oppose the treatment of republican women prisoners, in particular the practice of strip searching. She has written a number of articles and essays on these subjects and holds a doctorate in the history of the encounter between English and Irish feminism during the years of 'the Troubles'. She taught Irish Studies for over a decade at various institutions, including Kilburn Polytechnic (now the College of North West London), Birkbeck, London Metropolitan, and Luton universities.

Photojournalist Joanne O'Brien has written a book on Bloody Sunday, 'A Matter of Minutes'. She is also co-author of a book on Irish women's emigration to Britain, 'Across the Water'. Widely published in books, newspapers and magazines, her work was included in the 'Faces of the Century' exhibition at the National Portrait Gallery. She has worked in China, the USA & Europe. www.joanneobrien.co.uk.

Ireland's Hidden Diaspora:

the 'abortion trail' and the making of a London-Irish underground, 1980-2000

Ann Rossiter

Photographs by © Joanne O'Brien

Iasc Publishing
London

Published by Iasc Publishing 2009
email: iascpub@yahoo.co.uk

Copyright © Ann Rossiter, 2009
All rights reserved

Photographs by Joanne O'Brien
www.joanneobrien.co.uk

Typesetting and cover design
by Free Thinking Design
www.freethinkingdesign.co.uk

Printed and bound in Great Britain
by Printondemand-worldwide.com

ISBN 978-0-9561785-0-3
British Library Cataloguing in Publication Data.
A catalogue record for this book is available
from the British Library.

This book is dedicated to all the women of the Irish Women's Abortion Support Group and the Irish Abortion Solidarity Campaign

CONTENTS

FOREWORD

by Ivana Bacik
Senator, Dáil Éireann, and Reid Professor of
Criminal Law, Trinity College, Dublin

Abortion was legalised in Britain in 1967. Every year since then, thousands of Irish women have travelled to clinics in London, Liverpool, and other British cities to obtain abortions denied to them at home. The Irish law on abortion is the most restrictive in Europe. Abortion is a criminal offence in Ireland under 1861 legislation, carrying a penalty of life imprisonment.

In 1983, the law on abortion became even more restrictive when the Republic of Ireland's Constitution was amended to make the right to life of 'the unborn' equal to that of 'the mother'. A pregnancy may only be terminated legally in order to save the life of the pregnant woman. There is no right to abortion in any other circumstance; even where a woman or girl has been raped or abused.

Despite this highly repressive law, abortion is a reality in the Republic. More than 150,000 southern women and girls have had abortions over the last forty years. Yet these women's stories are never told publicly in Ireland. The cultural taboo on speaking out about abortion and crisis pregnancy has been strengthened by the intimidatory tactics of the anti-choice campaigners. Abortion represents their last line of defence since contraception and divorce were legalised. These conservative lobbyists have brought disproportionate influence to bear on fearful politicians.

But the tide is turning. At least now it is legal in Irish law to provide women with information on how to obtain abortion in Britain. This was not always so.

In 1989, I was elected President of the Students' Union at Trinity College Dublin. At that time, students' unions were the only organisations still publicly providing information about how to access abortion in Britain, after anti-choice groups had closed down women's counselling centres. In carrying out Union policy by giving information on abortion to women with crisis pregnancies, my fellow Union officers and I were threatened with prison by SPUC (the Society for the Protection of the Unborn Child) in a marathon court case. Mary Robinson (later elected President of Ireland) stepped in to defend us in court, and we were not sent to prison, but we lost our case initially and were threatened with bankruptcy.

The case made headlines in 1989 and 1990, and dominated the time I spent with the Students' Union. As one of the more publicly visible officers, I became the recipient of vitriolic hate mail, was verbally abused by strangers on the street, and encountered opposition even within the students' movement; not everyone was supportive of the principled stand the Union had taken.

After what can only be described as a difficult year in the Union, I escaped to London to do postgraduate work. During the previous twelve months, I had been deeply moved by the many phone calls I and other officers had taken from women with crisis pregnancies, unable to access the contact details for clinics in Britain and desperate to obtain this information from any source they could. In trying to help them as best we could, we students had become aware of a group of Irish women living in London who offered support, accommodation and assistance to women who had travelled there to seek abortions. This group was called IWASG (Irish Women's Abortion Support Group), and as soon as I arrived in London I made contact with them and offered to help.

The group was immediately welcoming and invited me along to their next meeting. The women who were there, mostly first and second generation Irish emigrants, were all remarkable individuals. As probably the youngest member at the time (I was then only twenty-two), and having arrived so recently from Ireland after the very difficult year we had had in the students' movement, I found it immensely empowering to meet so many unashamedly strong, liberated, pro-choice women – all with an Irish cultural background. I greatly valued the friendships I made within the group, which have been strong and long-lasting.

During the three years I lived in London, I became very involved with the work of the group. I attended regular meetings, helped to organise fundraising events, and contributed to supporting individual women who had travelled from Ireland for abortions; by meeting them, putting them up in my London flat, and sometimes escorting them to the clinic they had booked.

I thought the work that IWASG did was enormously important. During the 1980s and 1990s, when abortion was regularly in the headlines in the Republic as different cases were taken and referendum campaigns fought, it was particularly difficult for women to undertake the journey to England. Often this was done in secrecy, with no support from home. The women in IWASG offered very necessary moral support and non-judgemental help to many of the women and girls who travelled. I saw at first hand just how much their work was appreciated.

Since my time with IWASG, the law on information, and public attitudes, have changed for the better in the Republic – even if the law on abortion itself remains highly restrictive. This change has come about as a result of the 1992 X case. The case arose when a fourteen year-old pregnant rape victim, known only as X, wanted to travel to England with her parents to terminate her pregnancy. The State tried to prevent her travelling abroad in order to stop her having the abortion. People were understandably horrified at this inhumane attitude to the girl's crisis. In the public outcry that followed, the Supreme Court ruled that because X was suicidal, the pregnancy posed a real and substantial risk to her life, so her pregnancy could lawfully be terminated, and she was able to travel to England.

Two referendums were passed later in 1992. The first allowed freedom of information and enabled us students, finally, to win our long-running legal case. The second referendum allowed the right to travel for women seeking abortions. A referendum seeking to overturn the X case by ruling out suicide risk was defeated.

In 2002, following more pressure from anti-abortion groups, yet another referendum was held to try and rule out suicide risk as a ground for abortion – but again this was, thankfully, defeated.

Since then, the law has remained stagnant, and women have continued to travel to Britain in their thousands. To try and bring about change, activists in the Republic have recently established the Safe and Legal (in Ireland) Abortion Rights Campaign (SLI), with the aim of legalising abortion. The campaign is supporting an important case being taken by three women, A, B and C, against Ireland before the European Court of Human Rights. The women argue that their human rights were breached because they were forced to travel abroad for abortions. This is the first direct challenge to Irish abortion law before the European court, and it could bring about radical legal change

The SLI campaign is also working to mobilise public support for the legalisation of abortion generally. Opinion polls show that support for legal abortion has increased significantly in recent years. As Irish society has changed and liberalised, most people have become more compassionate towards women with crisis pregnancies.

The only thing that has not changed is the lack of courage and leadership demonstrated by successive Governments in failing to deal with abortion in a realistic and rational way. I believe that it is now time for women in Ireland to challenge the culture of silence and hypocrisy. We must press legislators to confront the reality of crisis pregnancy.

In this campaign for change, we should take inspiration from the work that the committed activists in IWASG and in the campaigning group Iasc have been doing for many years. Their stories, as told in this important book by Ann Rossiter, should provide a valuable source of motivation for the many women who believe, as I do, that it is time for change; time to meet the real health needs of Irish women by legalising abortion in Ireland.

FOREWORD

by Goretti Horgan
Alliance for Choice, Derry, Northern Ireland

The law on abortion in Ireland, North and South, is based on the same piece of Victorian legislation – the 1861 Offences Against the Person Act, which criminalizes abortion and lays down life imprisonment as the punishment. In Northern Ireland, the law has been updated somewhat by the 1937 'Bourne judgement' – the acquittal of a doctor who in England had performed an abortion on a fourteen year-old pregnant girl as a result of multiple rape. The core of the judgement is that abortion is legal if continuing pregnancy would leave the woman 'a mental or physical wreck'.

The Bourne judgement is notoriously unclear, which is why the 1967 Abortion Act was introduced in Britain. Both the (Westminster-appointed) Standing Advisory Commission on Human Rights and the UN Committee overseeing the Convention for the Elimination of Discrimination Against Women (CEDAW) have criticised Westminster for allowing the lack of clarity to persist in the North and for not acting to end the 'one law for the rich, another for the poor' situation.

The lack of clarity in the North was demonstrated when, between 1993 and 1995, four cases on abortion were considered by the Northern Ireland High Court in Wardship proceedings, in each of which permission was given for terminations to be carried out on the basis that the girls and women in question were under-age or legally incapable of consenting to the operation, and that their mental and/or physical health was at risk. These judgements suggest that abortion is legal in Northern Ireland in many more circumstances than is generally realised. It would seem that a large proportion of the women who travel to England for abortions would have a legal right to obtain them within Northern Ireland. Unfortunately, as in the South, doctors are afraid to carry out abortions for 'social' reasons although, unlike the South, it is acknowledged that between seventy and one hundred abortions are carried out in the North every year. Most of these are because the woman's life is in danger or for reasons of foetal abnormality: the abortions carried out for the latter reason are certainly illegal.

The law in the North is, then, a mess, and it's vulnerable women who are made to pay the price.

Established in the late 1990s, Alliance for Choice (AfC) is a broad-based non-funded organisation of women and men, Protestant and Catholic, campaigning for the extension of the 1967 Abortion Act to Northern Ireland and thereby putting an end to this mess. AfC was the result of the convergence of the Right to Choose Group in Derry, in existence since 1986/7, and the remnants of NIALRA, the Northern Ireland Abortion Law Reform Association, based in Belfast and dating back to the late 1960s, which began to wind up in the mid-1990s. AfC is supported by the major trade unions and has activists in most parts of the region – from Newry to Enniskillen, Belfast to Derry and most points in between.

AfC has, of necessity, focused mainly on helping get the money together for abortions in Britain and, increasingly, in Holland and Belgium where the procedure costs considerably less. The work has always been difficult and frequently stressful, and would have been impossible to maintain without the support and assistance of the Irish Women's Abortion Support Group, to whom many Irish women will be forever grateful.

If you've never left Ireland before, having someone to meet you in London and, for example, help you negotiate the Tube, it is a huge relief. Many women came back and told us that being able to stay with someone who 'knows the score' helped them greatly to get through the experience. A combination of cheap flights, internet access and changes to the regulations in Britain means it is now possible to Google the information, make an appointment with a clinic, travel, have an abortion and return to Ireland on the same day. As a result, IWASG is no longer as necessary as it once was. But it is still sometimes needed.

Most of AfC's early campaigning work was at the beginning of New Labour's period in government when many believed that the Labour Party would implement its promise to extend the Act. Instead, it became clear that during the negotiations on the 1998 Peace Agreement a deal had been done with the local political parties NOT to extend the Act. Concern for women's rights was discarded again in 2008 when Gordon Brown and Ian Paisley's Democratic Unionist Party (DUP) negotiated an arrangement whereby the DUP voted at the Westminster Parliament for 'terrorist' suspects to be detained without charge for forty-two days in return for New Labour scuppering any attempt to extend the Abortion Act to Northern Ireland. This is but one more example of draconian measures being taken under the smokescreen of 'security' and 'anti-terror'.

As well as working to get the Act extended, Alliance for Choice aims to 'tell the truth about abortion', to counteract the lies of the anti-abortionists. We want people in Northern Ireland to stop pretending we 'don't want abortion here' while approximately 1,500 women giving Northern Irish addresses access an abortion in Britain each year. Many more may give false British addresses or travel to Europe. Attitudes to sex have changed hugely in recent years and are now broadly similar to those in Britain. Sex is no longer confined to marriage: in 2007, almost six out of every ten babies born in Belfast were to mothers who were not married, although three out of four of these babies' births were registered by the two parents. Most women want to limit the number of children they have, but even the most reliable form of contraception has a two per cent failure rate. Consequently, not every woman is lucky enough to go through life without falling pregnant at a time when continuing the pregnancy would be difficult and even a disaster for her life.

Most people in Northern Ireland think that abortion in Britain is available free to Northern women on the National Health Service. Many women only discover that this isn't the case when they need an abortion. Even republican women who say they want nothing to do with anything British commonly respond to the discovery of this situation with – 'But we're part of the UK, it must be legal'.

Thus, for women without complicating medical conditions and with credit cards that are not maxed-out, terminating an unwanted pregnancy need not be such a big problem. Getting hold of between £500 and almost £2,000 depending on the length of the pregnancy may not be such a big deal for those with considerable financial resources at their disposal. However, for those not in such fortunate circumstances it is a huge problem. Today in Northern Ireland, working-class women may not be forced to go to backstreet abortionists, but they are forced to go to backstreet moneylenders for abortions that would be free on the National Health Service if they lived in Scotland, England or Wales.

Some women living on benefits or in the lowest-paid jobs simply cannot get the money together and are forced to continue unwanted pregnancies – even when the pregnancy is the result of rape. Lately, poorer women have been going on the internet and getting the abortion pill to cause an abortion themselves. If something goes wrong and they are caught by the authorities, theoretically they face life imprisonment.

In Northern Ireland we are now told that as a result of the Peace Agreement legal and political responsibility for abortion is to pass from Westminster to the Northern Irish parliament – the Assembly – whose seat is at Stormont. This means putting women's rights in the hands of an evangelical Taliban. Under Assembly rules, each of the two main parties (currently the Democratic Unionists and Sinn Fein) has a veto over legislation. Iris Robinson is a Member of Parliament at Westminster and a Member of the Legislative Assembly for the biggest party, the DUP. She is Chair of Stormont's Health Committee and so has some responsibility for the health needs of lesbians and gay men and, of course, the abortion issue. She caused an uproar in June 2008 when she told a BBC radio programme that homosexuality is a 'disorder' and recommended that gays see a psychiatrist. She told a House of Commons committee at Westminster that 'there can be no viler act, apart from homosexuality, than sexually abusing innocent children', a comment which was recorded in Hansard.

As a result of court cases taken by the Family Planning Association, the Department of Health for Northern Ireland was forced to issue guidelines to clarify to medical staff when abortion is legal in the region. After several years of prevarication, the guidelines were issued in January 2007: they allowed abortion when a woman's mental or physical health is in 'grave' danger of 'serious and permanent damage'. In autumn 2007, the Assembly rejected these as being too liberal.

A new set of guidelines, allowing abortion only if a woman's life is in immediate danger, was issued during the summer of 2008. The Assembly's Health Committee response to the new wording was agreed without any evidence of dissension from, for example, Sinn Fein members. It began by endorsing the views of the Association of Catholic Lawyers in Ireland – an organisation whose views make some of Iris Robinson's seem liberal.

It is clear that the Assembly will allow abortion only in the very limited circumstances that evangelical Protestantism and conservative Catholicism allows. The question which arises concerns what can be done in this situation to advance the right of women in the North of Ireland to self-determination, to control over their own bodies, and to the same level of health care as women in Scotland, England and Wales.

A successful outcome to the Southern Irish A, B and C cases in the European Court of Human Rights would be a victory for Northern Irish women as well. AfC is considering other legal routes, too. One would involve testing the law by carrying out medical abortions (i.e. using the drugs

Mifepristone, also known as RU486, and Misoprostol), by implication challenging the Public Prosecution Service and/or the courts to take action or concede that such abortions were legal.

The publication of this book will give our campaign another shot in the arm. It will both remind us of how bad it can get, and of the need to keep on keeping on until women in Ireland, North and South, have won for themselves the right to choose.

INTRODUCTION

Keeping secrets

Irish society needs women's silence to keep its good opinion of itself. In all the talk and high rhetoric of the endless abortion debate, the story of Irish women is usually authored by someone else, with few women daring to speak for themselves, to become visible.

Maeve Ruane[1]

This book is an oral history, not of abortion seekers themselves who have yet to speak in their own name, but of the London-Irish women who supported numbers of them over two decades, and who campaigned to change the law in both parts of the island. The supporters and campaigners in question were members of the Irish Women's Abortion Support Group (IWASG) and the Irish Abortion Solidarity Campaign (Iasc – *iasc* is the Irish word for 'fish'). The groups were part and parcel of what was called counter-cultural, sometimes Left-wing, sometimes anarchist, and always radical alternative or 'new wave'[2] (borrowing the term from the French cinema's *la nouvelle vague*) upsurge in Irish circles in Britain around feminist, gay and lesbian, anti-imperialist, and anti-racist issues. Although some of these groups were formed in the early 1970s, this book concentrates on the period extending from the early 1980s to the turn of the century.

Apart from occasional small bursaries, IWASG and Iasc remained entirely independent politically and financially throughout their existence. However, as will be seen in the following pages, IWASG received practical help from British health and welfare organisations, such as Women's Health and Release, and from members of the Spanish Women's

Abortion Support Group (SWASG) in London. Membership of IWASG was on two levels; at one level there were those offering accommodation only to abortion seekers, the other was made up of those also willing to attend meetings, and be involved in fund-raising and other activities. Both IWASG and Iasc were non-judgmental, members being in support of a woman's right to choose to have an abortion – or not.

Nobody is sure of the precise date when IWASG came into being; some founder members suggest 1980, others 1981. The inauguration date of Iasc is more precise. The campaigning group was formed in 1990 following a picket of the Irish Embassy in London over restrictions imposed by the Republic's Supreme Court on the provision of the names, addresses and telephone numbers of abortion clinics abroad. IWASG has now been wound down – not completely shut down – as the Irish 'abortion trail' has become a well established phenomenon requiring less in the way of support services at the British end.

Although never easy to negotiate, this trail, as Goretti Horgan has pointed out in her Foreword, has been assisted by the advent of the internet, 'the information highway'. The removal in 2001 of the legal requirement that non-resident women remain overnight in Britain following their abortion has helped, as has the era of cheap flights. Invariably, these developments have elicited a welcome sigh of relief from former members who, to a woman, have exclaimed: 'Redundant at last!'

Iasc's activities had also gone into decline, but, as discussed in Chapter 8, the rump of the group went into action again in the autumn of 2008. This action was in support of the British Member of Parliament (MP) Diane Abbott's amendment to the Human Fertilisation and Embryology Bill calling for extension of the 1967 Abortion Act to Northern Ireland, a move which was ultimately filibustered.

Essentially, this book is intended as a contribution to breaking the silence and challenging the taboo pervading the subject of abortion seekers (whether Irish or non-Irish residents) in Ireland itself, but also that prevailing amongst many Irish organisations in Britain. From the latter, one often hears the plea: 'We can't talk about or engage with the issue of abortion seekers from Ireland because it doesn't fall under our remit/would affect our funding/affect relations with the Irish government/infringe our charitable status/be too divisive', etc., etc. The book is also a testament to those who have provided material and emotional support for women in flight, as well as campaigning relentlessly for the right of women to reproductive choice at home in Ireland. In fact, this is the first time that many supporters and campaigners speak out without using pseudonyms.

Considerable effort has been made to avoid the book becoming another academic treatise. It shies away from the specialised language and concepts which make scholarly work difficult to tap into by many outside the 'charmed circle' of the academy. Much of the text is the spoken word, so consequently the 'essence' of things is not captured in a single word, in a pithy analogy, or metaphor, but more in people's ruminations on the subject. In fact, a regular comment about the text is that 'the quotations tend to drift a bit', which if translated means 'the book needs a good editor'. What is forgotten, perhaps, is that ruminations can be serendipitous.

Neither is this book written as a formal report, since the Irish landscape is peppered with reports on reproductive rights – or the lack of them. Amongst those gathering dust and growing musty on library shelves is the Republic's own Department of Health and Children's *Women and Crisis Pregnancy*[3] published in 1998. Furthermore, the debate on the pros and cons of abortion *per se* is not included. Acres of newsprint, as well as radio and television programmes in Ireland, Britain, the USA, and elsewhere have explored the subject at great length. The internet, too, has a proliferation of websites, such as *SPUC* and *Catholics for a Free Choice*, debating both sides of the argument. The complexities of the law, north and south of the border, are also debated at length on the web.

A number of awkward questions are raised for which there are no easy answers. The most difficult of these by far is the issue of the silence. In respecting abortion seekers' right to confidentiality, was it necessary that IWASG maintain a semi-underground state of existence in London? Did this mean pandering to the unspoken wishes of the two Irish states and many Irish community organisations in Britain? Another issue which pops up at various intervals in this book is the thorny question of whether voluntary support work is not just a form of sisterhood, but also an act of philanthropy with all the connotations that it implies. In consequence, does such an act feed into the myth of Ireland as an abortion-free zone by letting governments north and south of the border off the hook?

Then, there is the question of why it is that Irish organisations in Britain have been silent on the issue of abortion seekers. It would be far too easy to blame this silence on some form of direct censorship by the Catholic Church, as well as the government of the Republic which has provided some funding for such organisations. The fact is that even where their contribution to Irish organisations was miniscule (or even non-existent) none, apart from a few, such as the London Irish Women's Centre and Action Group for Irish Youth, have even acknowledged the subject of abortion. In fact, many Irish organisations have been in receipt of considerable funding from British sources which, more often than not, have embraced a policy of a 'woman's right to choose', the Greater London Council being a prime example.

From interviews and discussions which took place in the preparation of this book, it became apparent that even where Irish government bequests form a minor part of an organisation's entire funding, it would appear sufficient to set in motion a process of censorship, or more correctly, self-censorship, where the subject of abortion is concerned. Under the policy of multiculturalism discussed in Chapter 3, the British state at both national and local level has turned a 'blind eye' to such a practice.

Making invisible groups and individuals visible, allowing the silenced to speak – in short, what has been variously called 'bottoms up' or 'history from below' – has been an important endeavour in popular, counter-cultural movements post-1968. An important account of Irish migrant women in Britain is the oral history compilation *Across the Water, Irish Women's Lives in Britain* by three London-Irish activists which was published in 1988.[4] Since then, there have been a number of articles, mostly by academics, who have included interviews with activists in their work.[5] However, in providing a detached and analytic understanding of the post-1968 decades, scholars are not always able to convey a sense of what things meant to activists in the heat of the moment, in essence, to individuals tapping into their own lived experience, which, as the Italian expression goes, they have 'on their skins'.

Through the lens of one of several true stories recounted in the following pages, 'Sure we're all paddies over here' in Chapter 1, the frequently fraught nature of the abortion seeker's journey from Ireland is related. It tells of a mother and daughter's trauma in being 'caught up in the conflict' on their journey from a staunchly Loyalist area of Belfast to London for an abortion. Chapter 2 attempts to place Irish things sexual in historical and political context, an endeavour which has preoccupied writers from James Joyce to Edna O'Brien and, lately, Anne Enright, amongst many others. Chapter 3 looks at the background to Irish community activism in Britain since the 1950s, and the emergence of an 'alternative Irish community' in which abortion support work became a reality. It also addresses the prickly issue of the British state's policy of multiculturalism and its impact on Irish community organisations. Chapter 4 enquires into the beginnings and bloodlines of IWASG, while Chapter 5 looks at the nuts and bolts of the support work. Chapter 6 debates perceptions of the Irish abortion seeker as a 'special case', perceptions often mired by negative stereotyping and essentialism which display scant regard for historical and political contexts. Chapter 7 focuses on IWASG members and their motivation for being in the group. Most of the women concerned were Irish, but several were supporters from British and Spanish organisations, such as Women's Health and the Spanish Abortion Support Group. Chapter 8 recounts the history of the Irish Abortion Solidarity Campaign (Iasc). In the Appendix, the 2000/1 survey conducted for Marie Stopes International *The Other Irish Journey* is reproduced.

As a long-time member of IWASG and Iasc and still in contact with a number of former activists, I have been able to get in touch with numbers of those involved with the two groups over the past decades. However, some have returned to Ireland, some have moved to North America, and even further afield, to Australia and New Zealand, without leaving their contact details. While their stories and their perspectives need to be recovered and added to those included here to achieve a more comprehensive picture, I feel reasonably confident that a representative sample has had their say in the following pages. In writing this account it has become clear that before memory fades and, indeed, the activists concerned fade away, the task of compiling an extensive record of Irish immigrant women's activities takes on a particular urgency. It becomes all the more important when considering that in this electronic age we leave few footprints.

While the text might not win the Plain English Campaign's Crystal Mark award, I have tried hard to make it readable. I take full responsibility for any errors made. However, if readers have quibbles or can suggest glaring errors that need correcting, or indeed, know of activists or activism not included here, please email me so that these might form part of any further edition of this book: iascpub@yahoo.com

I would like to thank everyone who contributed to the book, particularly the members of IWASG and Iasc without whose contributions *Ireland's Hidden Diaspora* could never have been written. Also, Isabel Ros and Blanca Fernandez, formerly of the Spanish Women's Abortion Support Group (SWASG), Noreen Byrne, formerly of the Well Woman in

Dublin and the National Women's Council, Audrey Simpson of the Northern Irish Family Planning Association, Angie Birtill and Brid Boland, formerly of the London Irish Women's Centre, Pat Thompson, formerly of Women's Health, Jeanne Rathbone of SHEELA-NA-GIG, Doris Daly, formerly of myriad Irish organisations, amongst them the Sugawn Kitchen and Theatre, Goretti Horgan of Alliance for Choice in Derry, as well as Ivana Bacik of the Safe and Legal Campaign in Dublin. Many shared their stories and their thoughts with me, while others provided valuable background information. I hope that their views have been represented accurately and sensitively.

A very special 'thank you' is due to the Women's Trust Fund and Amanda Sebestyen of the Network for Social Change for making funding available for the publishing of the book. This meant that mainstream publishers did not have to be approached, since doubtless they would have insisted on curtailing the oral contributions, before even considering publication. To Mary Rochford, author of the collection of short stories, *Gilded Shadows*,[6] who shared with me her experiences of the publishing business, a special thanks.

Also, a vote of thanks needs to be given to Joanne O'Brien whose photographs grace the cover and pages of the book. Ros Scanlon, former Artistic Director of the Hammersmith Irish Cultural Centre, gave the project a necessary shot in the arm by encouraging me to do some readings from it at the 2008 Irish Bookfair at the Centre when the project was still in its infancy. 'Thank you', Ros, for your support and cheery words of encouragement on Friday mornings at the Older Irish Women's Drama Group at the Centre. Then, there were several interviewees who informed the sections of the book on the workings of the Irish community in Britain, including Patricia McCarthy at my local hairdressers in Northfields, West London. Although I have quoted only one contributor who wishes to remain anonymous, I would like to express my gratitude to them all.

Reading and editing tasks of all or parts of the book were undertaken by Eamer O'Keeffe, Bid Barnett, Noreen Byrne, Ann Hayes, Mary Sexton, Angie Birtill, Ellen Mullin, Mary Tyler, Marian Larragy and Gautam Appa. What can I say, other than a frivolous sounding 'thank you' and tell you how much I appreciate that you were there when the need was great. Marie Stopes International's consent to the inclusion in this book (as an appendix) of the survey conducted in 2000/2001 by Mary Sexton and myself, is also gratefully acknowledged. Finally, it is difficult to evaluate all that Gautam Appa, my partner, has done, since he was involved at every stage over the fifteen months during which this book, or indeed, what became this 'ogre', took over our lives.

Ann Rossiter
London, 2009

CHAPTER 1

Just Another Crisis Pregnancy

'Sure we're all Paddies over here'[1]

A fraught phone call from Heathrow at around 9 a.m. intrudes on a leisurely Saturday breakfast and newspaper-reading session. A hysterical voice in a strong Northern Irish accent says that someone needs to get to the airport – and quick. 'Me and me wee daughter are being held here', she says in a rush. 'They're holding us under the PTA (Prevention of Terrorism Act) and they say we need someone to vouch for us'. After a strong intake of breath, the woman gives her name and haltingly explains that she has brought her daughter to London for an abortion.

This is a new one for the listener. For years as a member of IWASG, the London-based Irish Women's Abortion Support Group, she has dealt with rape and incest scenarios and all manner of crises facing women who decide to terminate their pregnancies. She has known of cases where abortion seekers missed their flights, having been held up in roadblocks during the Orange marching season, or following IRA bombs in the North. But this case takes the biscuit. It certainly puts a new twist on what we euphemistically call 'the Troubles'. 'Talk about being caught up in the conflict', she thinks. 'Who knows, maybe this will throw a new light on what's known as being on the run!'

After putting the phone down the IWASG woman takes off at speed to catch the Piccadilly Line tube for Heathrow. She proceeds apace through the station barrier and along the seemingly endless corridor to the airport. 'Good for the figure, bad for the blood pressure', she muses as she finally arrives at the Information Desk at Terminal 1. She decides she must act calmly and decisively. 'Where can I find out about two women on a flight from Belfast being detained here under the PTA?' she asks the receptionist on the desk. 'Maybe it's the Airport Police, I need.' The woman doesn't answer at once, since it's hardly one of the ten or so most common questions she is posed on a daily basis. Covert looks are expressed while passing the details of the enquiry and the enquirer's ID down the line. Not surprising really, since for the duration of 'the Troubles', and even beyond, the general profile of all Irish people in Britain has been 'suspicious'. 'Good job I remembered to bring my passport', jokes the IWASG woman, trying to ease the tension. She gets a blank look in response.

Finally, the IWASG woman comes face-to-face with a police officer and explains at least twice over what she'd come for. Once again, she's asked to confirm her identity. Her passport ID is cross-checked with her driving licence and credit cards. The policeman seems to have difficulty figuring out the purpose of the detainees' visit. 'What do you mean, they're here for an abortion?', he argues, clearly unaware of the fact that abortion is to all intents and purposes illegal in Northern Ireland, as it is in the Republic, and that many thousands of Irish women pass through the airport each year to exercise their reproductive rights, albeit 'across the water'. It may well be legal, you might say, but it's hardly above board, given that Ireland's good opinion of itself depends on women keeping 'shtum'.

The policeman describes this state of affairs as 'quaint', when in fact he means 'archaic', for him proof of Catholic (curiously, he doesn't mention Protestant) Ireland's unwillingness to make an accommodation with women's rights, and its predilection for dumping its social problems on 'dear old Blighty'. He's right, of course. The spectacle of thousands of women having to make this trip each year – Ireland's 'hidden diaspora' – is both shameful and demeaning for many Irish and for those living in Ireland who define themselves as British. For others, it's crucial that the Emerald Isle remains forever a bastion of saints and scholars, a place which Samuel Beckett describes as imbued with the 'unrelieved immaculation' of heavenly ideals.

However, getting back to the unrelieved nastiness of base reality, the IWASG woman decides that rather than have a barney about history, politics, religion and the finer points of the colonial experience which have got the Irish into this morass, she'd better do something to get these women out of a fix. Mustering as much gravitas as she can under the circumstance, she keeps reminding him that he could verify the facts by the simple act of ringing the clinic. This, neither he nor his colleagues have so far been minded to do.

After a long wait, two ashen-faced women are released from detention. Over a cup of tea the mother tells how they boarded the first flight out of Belfast that morning and were detained as they passed through the unrestricted lane at Passport Control. The only explanation offered by the police for their detention was that they appeared agitated and looked 'fishy' in their black leather jackets. She had got the IWASG telephone number from a friend 'who'd been in a spot of bother', as she described it, and kept it in case of an emergency. She called it when she feared that she and her daughter would be put on a return flight to Belfast that morning.

The daughter remains silent, clearly traumatised by the ordeal. The mother repeats over and over, 'But I kept telling them (the police) that we're from…(a fiercely Loyalist enclave in Belfast). Don't they know we're not IRA, don't they know we're British? They just don't get it.' Without really thinking, the IWASG woman replies: 'Of course, they don't. Sure we're all Paddies over here'.

Her accent is unmistakably 'deep South', signalling alien territory to a Loyalist. Worse still, she's bound to be a papist. But the mother just blinks, and decides to say nothing, knowing that 'needs must when the devil drives'. In any case, the contradictions are too many.

This is a true story of a crisis pregnancy, unplanned, and unwanted in the mid-1990s. It is also a story of Loyalists[2] unwittingly caught in the fault lines of empire and war, of nationality and ethnic stereotyping. Being called a Paddy[3] is shocking for somebody who never really thought of herself as Irish, who never thought such a term of abuse applied to her. Then, there is the incongruity of having to pursue a termination available to her British compatriots across the water, but not on her own turf. Finally, there is the indignity of having to be rescued from the clutches of what she sees as her own security services by none other than a real Paddy, and not even a 'plastic'[4] one at that.

Other abortion seekers have been stopped and occasionally detained for questioning at the airports and sea ports, and at road checkpoints in Northern Ireland following bombing incidents, or during the Orange[5] marching season. More often than not, these have been Catholics who may have been nationalists or republicans.[6] Regardless of the specifics of this, and of all the other abortion stories, a number of common threads run through most of those recounted to IWASG volunteers. These almost always boil down to the myriad problems encountered once a woman decides she is unable or unwilling to go ahead with her pregnancy; accessing the relevant information to have a termination, making arrangements, finding a considerable sum of money at short notice or going into debt, undertaking a clandestine journey, and adopting a strategy of silence and subterfuge.

The fear of being found out, and the need to find a plausible excuse to cover an absence, whether from school, college, work, home, or childcare, is paramount. Also crucial is having a credible cover story at the ready in the event of running into acquaintances, friends, or even family, en route, at the airport, or even on the flight. Certainly, the two Loyalist women detained under the PTA will have prayed for an uneventful exit to Belfast. Almost certainly to the world at large they will have maintained complete silence about their ordeal on their return home. Chances are they will never speak of it again, even between themselves, eerily evocative of the wary resurfacing of Northern Irish paramilitaries after a sojourn 'on the run'. Undoubtedly, the consequences of keeping quiet will weigh heavily on their shoulders. How heavily is anyone's guess. Pro-choice proponents insist that it is the shame and subterfuge that make such women suffer longer and harder than they should. Opponents insist that women are always hurt by the abortion experience because it violates nature, motherhood, and God's purpose.

The women in question will have had sleepless nights worrying over the information gleaned during their encounter with the security services. They will have agonised over the fact that such details will have been entered on the Police National Computer as a matter of routine, available at the click of a computer mouse to their own police force, the Royal Ulster Constabulary (now the Police Service of Northern Ireland, PSNI). The termination itself will have been recorded in the figures for Northern Ireland required by British law to be furnished by the abortion providers, whether private clinics or National Health Service hospitals, and published annually by the Office of National Statistics. Yet, apart from the encounters with the police, with clinical staff, and the IWASG volunteer, such politically charged and acutely paradoxical incidents remain unmarked. This holds true whether in accounts of Irish people's experience of anti-terrorism legislation in Britain, in reports of Irish women's state of health, and indeed, in the annals of the movement of people across the Irish Sea.

In search of Irish abortion seekers in 'dear old Blighty'[7]

The fact that abortion is illegal except in rare cases in both the Republic of Ireland and Northern Ireland, and that a ban on the dissemination of information, whether verbal or in print, was imposed in the Republic between 1986 and 1995 might be sufficient grounds for disquiet amongst the more than million-strong Irish-born population of Britain and their children, whatever their personal views on abortion itself. However, the bizarre state of affairs is that in response to the ban, the movement each year of between five and six thousand abortion seekers giving Irish addresses from the Republic and fifteen hundred from Northern Ireland,[8] in and out of London and other major cities of Britain, has been largely unmarked. Even worse, these figures are likely to be conservative, as there is considerable anecdotal evidence that many give false British addresses and are included in the statistics for England and Wales.

When the phenomenon of what the British-based Irish writer, Marella Buckley, rather dramatically refers to as 'whole sectors of the Irish female population [who] pass through a secret tunnel to sexual amnesty and asylum'[9] is raised in Irish circles, whether at polite dinner parties or in the pub, it has too often become the elephant in the room. It is met with an embarrassed silence, or worse; 'I have problems with the idea of abortion, you know, it's not something I would opt for' type of response, as if we are talking of a matter of individual choice, rather than a significant Irish invisible export from two states where the notion of choice is hypothetical.

A similar situation prevails in the press and in scholarly documentation of the Irish. Regular news items do indeed appear in Irish newspapers in Britain, such as the *Irish Post* and the *Irish World*, but it has often been the case that these restrict themselves to quoting the latest figures produced by the Office of National Statistics for women crossing the Irish Sea for terminations. However, as pro-choice activists have strongly argued in the pages in the *Irish Post*, the real flesh-and-blood women behind these cold statistical facts – 'Ireland's hidden Diaspora' – and the reasons for their lonely journey, need to be fleshed out and discussed,[10] a move which looks like light years away if account is taken of the *Post*'s coverage of the amendment to the Human Fertilisation and Embryology Bill put down by Diane Abbott MP in October, 2008. If anything, the coverage of this event in the *Post*'s 25th October 2008 edition, save for a few local details, might have been lifted directly from the Vatican's *L'Osservatore Romano*. So much for a community newspaper attempting to give an unbiased account on the basis that its readership in this day and age is no longer monolithic!

Bearing in mind that it is often the case that the issue of reproductive rights, and reproductive health generally, assumes an importance in Irish women's lives at least as great as the 'grand narratives' of, say, nation and class, the eloquence of this silence is telling. The silence is even more surprising, given that abortion has been one of the most hotly debated and controversial issues in public life in the Republic of Ireland – if not in Northern Ireland – since the early 1980's. In the case of the Republic, it has been the subject of legal and political battles polarising society in a manner not experienced since the Civil War. One writer has even called it 'the second partitioning of Ireland.'[11]

CHAPTER 2

Putting Irish things sexual into context

Some people can even move their ears, either one at a time or both together. Others without moving the head can bring the whole scalp – all the part covered with hair – down toward the forehead and bring it back again at will...We observe then that the body...is an obedient servant...If this is so, is there any reason why we should not believe that before the sin [original sin] and its punishment of corruptibility [the Fall], the members of a man's body could have been the servants of man's will, without any lust, for the procreation of children?...because he did not obey God, [man] could not obey himself.

St. Augustine,
Father of the Christian Church[1]

It is not true that Christianity brought self-control and asceticism to a pagan world that delighted in pleasure and the body. Rather, hostility to pleasure and the body are a legacy of Antiquity that has been singularly preserved to this day in Christianity.

Uta Ranke-Heinemann,
Professor of Catholic theology[2]

I don't happen to regard sex between consenting adults as an occasion for punishment. Sex is not one of my guilt triggers.

June Levine, founder member of the
Irish Women's Liberation Movement[3]

The fraught question of what it is about Ireland, North and South, Catholic and Protestant, that makes for such an anomaly when it comes to human sexuality and reproductive matters, has bewildered many, not least on the island of Ireland itself. Is it all down to religion, the original culprit being the ascetic, self-denying and austere monasticism with pre-Christian roots common in Ireland in the fifth century and later? Did this repressive regimen, with its strong emphasis on sexual restraint, come to be bolstered by the Augustinian fixation with original sin? Was it all about Eve, the seducer of man, the sinner who lost the Garden of Paradise for all of humanity that has left such a legacy of misogyny in Christianity? Further, was the situation exacerbated by the arrival of Jansenism (a strict form of Augustinianism) introduced into the Irish Catholic underground church in the dark era of the Penal Laws?

Moving on to the nineteenth century, in the making of this anomaly, what part was played by Irish nationalism in its response to British colonialism? Unlike other Catholic countries of Europe, notably France, Italy and Spain, why has there been no anti-clerical movement in Ireland? What of the role of economics, especially following the Great Famine, known as *An Gorta Mór* (the 'Great Hunger' or 'Great Starvation') of 1845-50? Out of a population of about eight millions, a million or so died, and between 1845 and 1870 it is said that about three million emigrated, a process which to a large extent wiped out the class of landless labourers. This left behind a society which came to be dominated by the 'strong farmer', more willing than the landless labourer to comply with the strictures of the economy, and, of course, the Church. The fear of famine (there were further failures of the potato crop, still the staple diet of Irish tenant farmers, in the late 1870s), having to choose between starvation, eviction, and, if they had the boat fare – emigration – which was the great underlying political reality of the late seventies and early eighties of nineteenth-century Ireland. These conditions vividly etched themselves on the minds of subsequent generations, making the catastrophe the main event in modern Irish history, as important to the Irish as the French Revolution is to the French, and the Cultural Revolution is to the Chinese.

What, then, were the precise conditions in which the Irish are regarded as having moved from being among the most (and earliest) married to among the least (and latest) married people in Europe, with over half of women between their mid-twenties and mid-thirties remaining spinsters as the nineteenth century came to an end, figures that had, in fact, increased by the time the Census of 1926 was taken? What was it about this new order of things which, in the words of one writer, made marriage a 'fundamentally unromantic' transaction 'arranged by a matchmaker, attended by endless negotiations and wranglings over dowry and worth' which eventually 'paired a girl of twenty with a man often well over forty.'[4] Why did it put an end to farmers' sons marrying loved ones '*gan bó, gan punt, ghan ábhar spré*' (without cow, pound, or dowry), and usher in an era where '*is mar gheall ar bhólach a phóstar mná*' (it is for the cows that women are married). Why was it that, once married, the Irish had larger families than many peasant societies in Europe at the time? What was the role of religion in policing the sexuality of the married and the single alike? Was there an unspoken and unwritten contract between the people and the Catholic Church on the matter of reproduction? And, how significant a contribution did emigration make in reducing the number of mouths to feed and getting rid of potential dissidents?

In other words, what are the strands of this complex web of historical, political, economic and cultural aspects of Irish society that make for understanding the way in which sexuality and reproductive choice have been viewed and controlled in Ireland? Trying to get to the bottom of it all, progressing beyond the crude interpretation that sees the Irish as faithful, if irrational, followers of religion – a trait said to flow freely in the Guinness if not the water supply – has been largely the preserve of the academics. Numerous works have appeared in recent years to help us make sense of it.[5] While Chapter 6 picks up on the differences between Catholicism in

Ireland and continental Europe, what follows is a look at the world of culture and the part it has played in illuminating some of the strands. Thereafter, is a brief outline of the theological origins of attitudes and beliefs towards sex and sexuality in the Irish tradition.

Making sense of it all – the role of culture

In 1974, the poet, Phillip Larkin, wrote in his *Annus Mirabilis* that 'sexual intercourse [or talk of it] began in nineteen sixty-three'. In and around the same time, Shelagh Delaney's play, *A Taste of Honey* (1958),[6] Bryan Forbes' film, *The L-Shaped Room* (1962) and Ken Loach's television docudrama, *Up the Junction* (1965), placed centre-stage the problem of unwanted pregnancy in Britain and acted as an important 'wake up' call. All three were shocking to contemporary audiences, and remind us today that mean-minded Victorian values laced with large doses of Christian morality were still far more prevalent in 1960s Britain than history now pretends. All three represented major contributions to a national debate on a difficult social issue of the time. The impact of *Up the Junction* was considerable. Its portrayal of backstreet abortion touched many viewers, made all the more poignant with the death of the protagonist undergoing a dangerous and illegal procedure.

Similarly, when Ireland's 'wake-up' call in the form of Edna O'Brien's first book, *The Country Girls* (1960),[7] appeared, it was immediately banned – and soon burned – in Ireland for its forthright portrayal of female sexual desire, its references to birth control, and to divorce. These were depicted in the naïve and reckless flirtations and passionate misadventures of the protagonists, Kate Brady and Baba Brennan. For Kate and Baba, caught up in the whirl of life under the bright lights of Dublin's fair city after freeing themselves from the constraints of rural Ireland, the threat of becoming 'preggers' forms a constant backdrop to the novel. When, in the sequel, *The Girl With Green Eyes* (1964),[8] Kate does cross 'the water' to London, it is to escape the wrath of the clergy and the physical threats of her father, both parties incensed by her pregnancy and shotgun marriage to a divorcee. At the time in Ireland, these were seen as offences against God and Mother Church.

More recently, audiences were reminded of the 'bad old days' by Mike Lee's film, *Vera Drake* (2005), with its realistic portrayal of the almost forgotten subject of back-street abortion set in Britain fifty or so years ago. The other was Cristian Mungiu's, *4 Months, 3 Weeks and 2 Days* (2007) which explored the grim realities of Ceausescu's mythical abortion-free Romania. A parallel film on the Irish state of affairs was *Hush-a-Bye Baby*, the 1989 feature made by the Derry Film and Video Workshop. The film garnered a slew of international film awards and was shown on television. However, its depiction of the failed home abortion of a 15-year old Derry girl met with outrage in Northern Ireland and ensured that the film never made it to cinema screens.

The publication of fiction and poetry exploring the issue has been more successful. At the height of political turmoil in the Republic when the provision of information on accessing an abortion was outlawed, Paul Durcan published a poem with the provocative and subversive title of *A Catholic Father Prays for His Daughter's Abortion* in his collection, *The Berlin Wall Café* (1985).[9] The poem speaks of a father's desire that his daughter be tended by compassionate nursing nuns while undergoing an abortion which he says is 'her due'. Even more poignant is Patricia McCarthy's poem, *Abortion* (1994),[10] which captures the raw and intense emotion felt by a woman during her termination, pondering, she says, the choice she did not have.

The issue has also been explored in Anne Enright's novel, *What Are You Like?* (2002)[11] and Maeve Binchey's short story, *Shepherd's Bush* in her collection, *Victoria Line, Central Line* (1978), in which May, the central character, speaks of the lonely, anxious trip to London less than an hour away from Ireland.[12] Joseph O'Connor's, *Cowboys and Indians* (1992),[13] also probes the subject. Surprisingly, the latter never translated to film, although it seems to have many ingredients appealing to a young audience like Roddy Doyle's highly successful book, *The Commitments* (1988),[14] which became a film with the same title.

Creative writing apart (as has been stated above – and is re-stated throughout this book), little has been said or written of first-hand experiences. The late June Levine, a Dublin journalist and one of the founding members of the Irish Women's Liberation Movement, is probably unique in writing a detailed account of a termination she had in London. While disclosing that she opposes abortion, she says she was not doused in guilt and fear, as are so many Irish women. This was possibly due to the influence of her Jewish father, given the fact that sex and sin do not have the same grim association in the Judaism of the Old Testament. In *Sisters, The Personal Story of an Irish Feminist*, Levine tussles with the fraught question of what it is that makes Ireland different from other European countries when it comes to human sexuality and reproductive matters. Sex, she argues, is a guilt trigger for Catholic Irish women and, even as late as 1982 when her book was published, she is forced to conclude that pregnancy was still often thought of as a punishment for sexual activity.

While not contesting Levine's conclusion, it needs to be emphasised that this guilt trigger is also commonplace amongst women in certain strands of Protestantism. Most importantly, it is prevalent in evangelical Presbyterianism, a belief system which is central to the structure of Northern Irish politics, and whose influence extends far beyond its membership.[15] The common thread running through the various brands of Christianity seems to lead us back to pre-Reformation days, in fact, to Antiquity, and subsequently to the teachings of St. Augustine, as well as his successors.

Sex as sin: St. Augustine et al

There is no doubt that someone who is seen as one of the first great Church Fathers, St. Augustine of Hippo in North

Africa who became a Christian in 387AD and died in 430 AD, has left a serious blot on the landscape of the Irish body, male and female, Catholic and Protestant. Although differing from some of his fellow theologians, Augustine radically separated love and sexuality and connected the transmission of something he invented called 'original sin', or what the Eastern Church calls 'ancestral sin', with the pleasure of intercourse. This belief derived from the view held in Antiquity by Plato, Pythagoras, and Aristotle, amongst others, that the sexual act was harmful to men in that it drained them of energy. More importantly, it caused them to lose self-control, as Augustine himself explains in the quotation at the outset of this chapter, where he argues that were it not for lust, the members of a man's body would obey his will.

The young Augustine (like so many young men and women before and after him), was clearly startled and deeply troubled by the strength of his sexual urges. In preparation for his conversion to Christianity at the age of twenty-nine, he summarily despatched the woman (he never disclosed her name) he had been living with for twelve years, deprived her of the son she had borne in the relationship, and, presumably had a part to play in the vow she made that she would never sleep with another man. However, writing in his *Confessions*, he claims he again became 'a slave to lust' and took another lover. Augustine was a member of the Manichees sect, founded by the Persian, Mani, said to have been born around 216 AD, which demanded a completely ascetic life from its followers and rated celibacy much higher than the married state.[16]

At best, the Manichees might be considered a bunch of cranks; at worst they might be seen as fanatics, especially nowadays. However, on his conversion, Augustine transmitted his Manichaeism to Christianity and given his hugely authoritative standing in the Church, the doctrine had a major impact. From the biblical story relating that when Adam and Eve disobeyed God and ate the forbidden apple, Augustine came to the conclusion that they were ashamed and covered their sexual parts with fig leaves. Sexual intercourse, or more precisely sexual pleasure, was for him the viaduct through which his invention, original sin, is transmitted from generation to generation. The exception was Christ who came into this world in a virginal birth: 'Christ was begotten and conceived without any fleshly pleasure and so he also remained free from every kind of defilement by original sin.'[17]

Augustine influenced leading divines who followed in his wake. Amongst these was another pre-eminent father of the Church, St. Thomas Aquinas (1224-74 AD), who viewed woman as a defective man and wrote in his *Summa Theologica* that she was 'conceived because of weakness in the seed, or because a damp south wind was blowing at the time'. Such misogyny has continued to flow in Christianity through the ages because of the notion that women represent sex, an occasion of sin – for men. Although he broke with Rome and instigated the great Reformation which shook Europe in the sixteenth century, the former Augustinian monk, Martin Luther, who married a nun and railed against celibate priests, nonetheless maintained the Augustinian link between sex and sin. Two major Reformation figures, John Calvin and Cornelis Jansen, were also followers of Augustine. Jansen was the father of a strict form of Augustinianism known as Jansenism, introduced into the Irish Catholic underground church in the dark era of the Penal Laws in the eighteenth century by Irish priests trained in continental seminaries. Also to be included in the band of Augustinian brothers was John Knox (the Scottish author of *The First Blast of the Trumpet Against the Monstrous Regiment of Women* published in 1558), who is still a major figure in Northern Irish Presbyterianism.

For Augustine, original sin meant eternal death which was redeemable only by God's grace through baptism. Unbaptised children were condemned to eternal death in the Limbo of Infants, a hypothetical afterlife, a place at the edge of Hell where the soul is denied the beatific vision, or sight of God. The German Catholic theologian, Uta Ranke-

Heinemann, points out that such was the impact of this theological position that in the twelfth century a bishop of Paris went as far as issuing a *fatwa*, or religious edict, ruling against dead pregnant women being laid out in church. Neither could they be buried in consecrated ground unless the foetus was cut from their body.[18]

Augustine had ordained that the sexual act had but one purpose, namely procreation, following from the biblical imperative to Adam and Eve to 'Go forth and multiply'. In his *De Conjugiis Adulterinis*, he stated: '...it is unlawful and shameful to have intercourse even with one's own wife if the conception of children is avoided.'. Augustine also set his face against abortion as did Aquinas who followed in his footsteps. However, both were of the belief that abortion was permissible up to the moment of 'ensoulment'. A male foetus was said to be animated or ensouled at about forty days after conception, and a female after ninety. In consequence, abortion was considered as murder only when a foetus was 'animated'.

Throughout the centuries the Augustinian doctrine on sexuality and marriage remained virtually unaltered until growing secularism and the development of more radical views amongst lay Christians challenged it and rendered it less convincing as the nineteenth century progressed. In the twentieth century, from the Catholic Church came the papal encyclical on marriage, *Casti Cannubi* (Christian Marriage), issued by Pius XI in 1930. However, this doctrine was neither fully accepted nor fully rejected.

The encyclical declared that love in Christian marriage held 'a kind of primacy of excellence', thus affording love a position it had never before held, and, as such, effecting a sort of break with Augustinian theory.[19] However, in restating its old position of sex for procreation only, and fertility to be limited by abstinence or use of the 'safe period', Catholics world-wide were thrown into confusion. One of the most glaring examples of the dithering and hypocrisy which ensued was the introduction to the Republic of Ireland of the birth control pill in 1962 as a 'menstrual regulator'.

Somehow, overnight, menstruating Irish women became the most irregular in the world, giving rise to a widespread questioning about the vagaries of their reproductive health!

Protestants differ from Catholics on the subject of contraception and the Anglican Church in Britain cautiously approved of it in 1930. However, it must be emphasised that it was not until 1958 that the ruling body of the Anglican Church, the Lambeth Conference, could declare that the use of contraception was entirely a matter for the individual conscience.[20] As far as abortion in the contemporary period is concerned, as with contraception, liberal Protestants are more likely to see it as a matter of individual conscience informed by reason. Evangelical or fundamentalist Protestant sects and the Catholic Church hold that human life begins at the moment of conception, and not at birth, hence there is unqualified official opposition. A further problem is that since 1983, when Pope John Paul II promulgated a new Code of Canon Law, a person who procures a successful abortion incurs automatic excommunication.

Infanticide versus Abortion in Ireland

An increasing amount of evidence is coming to light to show that historically Irish women used various means to end unwanted pregnancies, whether through abortion, infanticide, concealment, or abandonment. They also gave their babies up for adoption, sometimes voluntarily but mostly not. The story of 'illegitimate' children, the adoption process, and, in many cases, their export to the USA and elsewhere, is only now beginning to be chronicled in full.[21] As far as the history of abortion in Ireland is concerned, in his account of Mamie Cadden, midwife and Ireland's most famous backstreet abortionist, Ray Kavanagh is at pains to point out that there were referral networks throughout Ireland and a not insignificant number of abortion practitioners in the 1930s, 40s, and 50s, many of them located in Dublin.[22] Rather tellingly, the greatest number of abortions are recorded as occurring during the Second World

War, a period when travel restrictions between Ireland and Britain were imposed. Even more telling, is the fact that a reduction in the numbers of abortions coming to the attention of the Irish police and the courts has been noted from the time the 1967 Abortion Act was passed in Britain.[23]

Ample evidence is available from police and criminal records to show that compared to Northern Irish, English, Welsh, or Scots, women in relatively greater numbers from the counties (predominantly Catholic) which ultimately made up the Republic, chose infanticide, concealment and abandonment of babies over abortion. This remained so at least until the 1967 Act came into force in Britain. The lower numbers in counties with a predominantly Protestant population are likely to support the fact that limbo was not such an issue for Protestants. This evidence is to be gleaned from a seminal study of fertility control in Ireland from the nineteenth century to the mid-1970s conducted by Richard Rose.[24] From his investigations, Rose concludes that, 'while Irish women have traditionally rejected the idea, to use the euphemism, of killing their babies before they were born, they have on the other hand killed and discarded them *after* they were born.'[25] He quotes from the Irish newspaper, the *Cork Examiner* of 9th October 1929 relating a judge's comments on the subject:

> *His Lordship, referring to cases of concealment of birth, said the number of newly-born infants in the country who were murdered by their mother at present surpassed belief. Only one out of fifty came up in the courts, but there was a wholesale slaughter of those innocents going on through the country, the means by which their bodies were disposed of being shocking to human nature.*

Even as late as 1984, two cases convulsed the southern Irish state in a frenzy of perdition. One of these was what became known as 'the Kerry baby', found on a beach in Cahirciveen, Co. Kerry, having been stabbed to death soon after birth. The other involved the concealment of the birth, death and burial on the family farm of Joanne Hayes' baby, in Abbeydorney, Co. Kerry.[26]

Why did so many Catholic Irish women chose infanticide, abandonment or concealment over abortion? A number of possibilities come to mind by way of explanation. First, there was lack of means to procure an abortion in a predominantly rural society under heavy surveillance by the priests of the parish, the police, and the neighbours (aka the 'neighbourhood watch'). Abortionists would have found it difficult to survive long in these conditions. Secondly, the pregnant rural woman might not have found it easy to tap into big city abortion networks. Even if she were able to do so, lack of money might deter her. For example, in all infanticide cases coming before the courts from the early 1920s to the late 1950s, it was noted by Alexis Guilbride in her essay, 'Infanticide, the Crime of Motherhood', that every woman was classified as 'poor or destitute' and almost all were unmarried.[27]

Thirdly, amongst rural and urban women alike, there was likely to be complete ignorance of how their bodies functioned. Even the most rudimentary sex education was unavailable, and it was not unknown for women to first learn they were pregnant as they went into labour and delivered. Fourthly, there was an over-riding fear of stigma attached to being an unmarried mother and to her child in a society that punished sexual 'deviancy' more harshly than most, the most extreme being banishment to the Magdalen Asylums.

Last, but not least, another reason for the choice of infanticide was that failure to baptise a foetus condemned its soul to reside in limbo, a belief transmitted from Augustine down through the fathers of the Catholic Church, despite there being no formal doctrine to the effect. Limbo, all Catholic children learnt from their Catechism, was 'a place or state of perpetual darkness' where the soul was forever denied sight of God and his grace. Such was the stigma attached that an unbaptised infant was traditionally buried in unconsecrated ground in what was known as a *kileen*. The pain and anguish so many generations of Catholic experienced when contemplating abortion is acutely expressed by Anne O'Connor, the Irish folklorist:

> *The fear of divine retribution for committing sin, and the agony for women who had to have abortions even though they knew they were thereby depriving their child of eternal life has been well documented [in folklore]. Many references to women trying to baptise the child or foetus in their womb, before having an abortion, exist*[28]

Epilogue: in limbo no longer

On the 20th April 2007, Pope Benedict XVI declared limbo defunct. Reversing traditional Roman Catholic teaching, Benedict approved a Vatican report which said that there were 'serious' grounds to hope that children who die without being washed clean of original sin through baptism can go to heaven. The declaration produced an eerie feeling in many Catholics, practising and lapsed, when reading newspaper reports of statements on the subject by theologians. One in particular stood out for its brevity and relaxed, even blasé tone, that of the Reverend Richard McBrien, Professor of Theology at the American Catholic University of Notre Dame, who said:

> *If there's no limbo and we are not going to revert to St. Augustine's teaching that unbaptised infants go to hell, we're left with only one option, namely that everyone is born in a state of grace. Baptism does not exist to wipe away the stain of original sin, but to initiate one into the Church.*[29]

By all accounts, no mention was made by the Reverend, or any other Vatican spokesperson, to the anguish suffered by generations of Catholic women the world over. No regrets or apologies either for women over the centuries being put through the ordeal of thinking their children were being deprived of eternal life. But no surprise there, since women have traditionally been considered the children of a 'lesser god' in the Catholic Church. In some ways this lack of remorse and tactlessness brings to mind the traditional Irish children's song about infanticide, *Weila, Weila Waile*, which children enthusiastically sang unaware of its dark meaning. Adults, too, sang it with abandon. The Dubliners, among many groups on the Irish traditional music scene, frequently gave renditions of it around the pubs and clubs of Ireland, as did the Clancy Brothers. The latter, it is said, referred to *Weila, Weila Waile* as a 'nice child's song' one might hear on the stairs of a Dublin tenement:

And there was an old woman and she lived in the wood
Weila, Weila Waile
There was an old woman and she lived in the wood
Down by the riverside*
Well she had a baby three months old
Weila, Weila Waile
She had a baby three months old
Down by the riverside
And she had a penknife long and sharp
Weila, Weila Waile
She had a penknife long and sharp
Down by the riverside
Then she stuck that penknife in the baby's heart
Weila, Weila Waile
She stuck that penknife in the baby's heart
Down by the riverside

*In some versions, this line is sung as 'down by the River Sáile'.

CHAPTER 3

'We were our bit of the Irish community': the making of the *alternative* Irish community in London.

Setting the scene

Oh Mary this London's a wonderful sight
With the people here working by day and by night.
They don't sow potatoes, nor barley, nor wheat,
But there's gangs of them digging for gold in the streets.
At least when I axed them, that's what I was told.
So I just took a hand at this diggin' for gold,
But for all that I found there, I might as well be,
Where the Mountains of Mourne sweep down to the sea.

From a ballad by Percy French

The drive for the setting up of support and campaigning groups for Irish abortion seekers came from women immigrants who arrived in Britain in successive waves in the 1960s, 1970s and 1980s. Most left Ireland when they were in their late teens or early twenties and a significant number settled in the south-east of England, particularly in London.[1] In the ranks of these support and campaigning groups there was also a sprinkling of second and third-generation Irish whose parents had settled in Britain in the 1950s and before. Invariably, group members were influenced by the radical social movements originating in France and Italy in the late 1960s. Most inspiring were the movements in the USA. These emerged from the drive for black civil rights and opposition to the Vietnam War, in the process fuelling a hurricane of protest worldwide. In fact, the former was one of the sparks that ignited the civil rights movement in Northern Ireland. There was also the powerful influence of feminism, itself a product of the civil rights and anti-war upsurges, a movement which began in America and soon spread across the globe. Some of the pro-choice supporters and campaigners had seen active service in the women's movement in Ireland itself, while others experienced feminism for the first time in Britain.

The world into which the activists were catapulted at the beginning of the 1980s was one of much excitement and euphoria, but also one of disappointment, pain and anger. Between 1981 and 1986, the Left had control of the Greater London Council (GLC) which was led by Ken Livingstone. Social movements like women's liberation, lesbian and gay liberation, anti-racism, and anti-imperialism were in ferment. More sombrely, the late 1970s and early 1980s saw uprisings of Afro-Caribbean and Asian Londoners in Brixton, Tottenham's Broadwater Farm, and Southall. Subsequently, the 'Iron Lady', Margaret Thatcher, embarked upon the Falklands War, and later, in 1984, brought the full force of the law and the constabulary to bear on the miners' strike. Perpetually, it seemed at the time, Northern Ireland loomed large in the backdrop to political life in Britain.

However interesting and exceptional this group of women activists might have been, they were likely to go more or less unmarked in the annals of the Irish in Britain if long-established tradition were to be followed. In fact, the first significant debate to be heard concerning Irish women of the diaspora occurred sometime in the early 1980s. Around that time photocopies of an academic tome made from the original housed in the US Library of Congress began to do the rounds of Irish feminist circles in London. The book, *Emigration, Marriage and Fertility*,[2] had been written by an American academic with the illustrious name of Robert Emmet Kennedy, and had been published way back in 1973.

Kennedy's study gave women pride of place, doubtless influenced by the burgeoning women's movement in the US at the time. He revealed that women had tended to dominate the outflow of Irish migration to Britain and the USA in most periods of the nineteenth and the twentieth century up to 1971. Other researchers who followed in his wake highlighted the fact that women's reasons for migrating did not always mirror those of their male counterparts. They have emphasised the staggering numbers involved, relieved only when Irish males left in large numbers, either to serve in the British army, or to fill jobs left by British army recruits in the two World Wars. Most shocking of all is the knowledge that reliable statistical evidence had been around since 1871, it was just that it seemed to pass government bodies and researchers by.[3]

Were it not for the rise of Irish feminism in Britain, this act of collective forgetfulness might have persisted. Irish migration was almost always seen as a 'man thing', dominated by the powerful imagery of the Irish navvy's Herculean prowess on Britain's highways and byways, whether in the building of bridges, canals, harbours, railways, reservoirs and roads from the second half of the eighteenth century to the present time. Such was the Irish navvy's distinction that a parody of the first Q&A of the Catholic Penny Catechism did the rounds in Irish circles in Britain. In an exchange between schoolboy and schoolmaster, it went as follows:

Who made the World?

McAlpine, sir![4]

Among the enduring memorials to the Irish navvy's toil are the London Underground, the M1 motorway, the Shell Building, the 'Chunnel' – the Channel Tunnel between England and France – and the South Bank concrete complex where four workers lost their lives in appalling working conditions.[5]

In America too, the image endured of the men who lived by muscle and guts. Such images were bolstered by exploits like those of the Molly Maguires, the secret society, set up in the 1870s by Irish miners brutalised and impoverished by the owners of the rich Pennsylvania coal fields. They are immortalised in James O'Neill's novel *The Molly Maguires*[6] and the Hollywood film of the same name starring Sean Connery and Richard Harris. More recently, the Irish protagonists in Martin Scorsese's film, *Gangs of New York*, gave further imaginative sustenance to such masculine derring-do.

In contrast, the men's female opposite numbers: the skivvy (the habitué of the English and American 'below stairs'), the washerwoman, and more recently, the hospital nurse, all represented the domestic, nurturing and private domains. This was hardly the stuff of tall tales told in pubs after a day's hard toil, however much back-breaking drudgery was involved, or sufficiently dramatic to be portrayed on film. Nor, indeed, was it the subject of migrant songs. In the old Percy French ballad quoted at the beginning of this chapter, it is the male immigrant who laments his fate in London, and it is his wife or lover, Mary, who plays the waiting game against the dramatic landscape of the Mountains of Mourne.

If female immigrants have suffered from invisibility in the history of the Irish in Britain, the presence of the Irish overall, male and female alike, has waxed and waned in the British historical narrative over the centuries. Invariably, this depended on the state of Anglo-Irish relations. During periods of conflict, such as the many Irish uprisings against British rule from the United Irishmen in 1798, the Fenians in the 1860s, and the Easter Rising in 1916, the Irish were marked out as a turbulent, troublesome and violent people.

The high visibility of the Irish in nineteenth-century Victorian Britain was also due to the mass influx of impoverished and often sick refugees as a consequence of the Great Famine. Residing mainly in already overcrowded and destitute slums in Britain's urban areas, the 'Famine Irish' were seen as the harbingers of disease, criminality, political violence, religious superstition in the form of papism, and any number of threats to civil society. Conversely, they had sunk almost without trace in official, academic, and popular accounts of the people of Britain during the first half of the twentieth century. This is despite large-scale migration from Ireland throughout the period.

The sidelining of Irish immigrants in the post-war period was in large measure due to the preoccupation of the press, politicians, and the hue and cry raised by the far-Right over the influx of West Indians, or 'Toasted Paddies' as they were disparagingly called. These came to bear the brunt of antagonism directed at foreigners on British soil, and supplanted the Irish at the bottom of the economic ladder. Focus on the Irish was further deflected when hostility towards the arrival of Indians and Pakistanis from the Indian sub-continent, and later from East Africa, began to career out of control as the 1960s progressed. The response to the newcomers in many sections of British society found resonance in Enoch Powell's 'rivers of blood' speech in 1968 as the era of 'Paki-bashing' was ushered in.[7]

The IRA's bombing campaign in Britain propelled the Irish population into stark relief once again, and created a sense of high tension in Irish circles. Hardly a month went by without news of another explosion and the attendant casualties, injuries, damage to property, as well as the inevitable disruption to traffic and transport communications.[8] Then, there were the arrests, detentions, and convictions of numerous Irish people in Britain, from which followed a series of miscarriages of justice, the Birmingham 6, the Guildford 4, the Maguire 7, and Judith Ward amongst them. The protests of the men and women prisoners in Northern Ireland's Long Kesh (The Maze) and Armagh Jail, and the deaths of ten men in 1981 following a hunger strike, all contributed to the climate of tension.

The Prevention of Terrorism Act (PTA), first introduced in 1974 in the aftermath of the Birmingham pub bombs, quickly transformed an invisible community to one which became demonised and 'suspect'. The PTA's wide powers of examination, arrest, and detention resulted in more than seven thousand people being held in police custody (over six thousand were released without charge) in the period 1974 to 1991.[9] The trawling of Irish neighbourhoods, like Kilburn in London, and the screening of passenger flows through the ports, ostensibly for information regarding IRA or INLA activity, caused considerable anxiety. Irish people, regardless of class and political perspective on 'the Troubles', came to experience fear and apprehension.

Political activity around the Irish National Question became dangerous. State censorship and self-censorship became the order of the day. Dissent was muffled, and the received wisdom is that the Irish in Britain 'kept their heads down' for the duration. Established Irish political and community organisations felt the heat, and many saw fit to maintain a low profile. Although there were always individuals who bucked the trend in the ranks of these groupings,[10] according to Michael Herbert in his history of the Irish in Manchester, the Federation of Irish Societies (formed in the early 1970s as an umbrella group which linked County Associations, Irish centres and Irish businesses) 'remained silent'.

Herbert argues that the Federation had 'a Catholic ethos and a welfare focus and was generally supported by the Irish government of whatever political hue.'[11] By all accounts, the Counties Associations gave a wide berth to issues related to 'the Troubles'. Founded mainly in the 1950s with the support of the Catholic Church, and with the aim of fostering links with immigrants' communities in Ireland, these adopted constitutions vetoing discussion of political matters.[12]

The prohibition of all things political had an earlier history stemming from the clergy's fear of the influence of the Connolly Association, a republican socialist organisation with links to the Communist Party. Since its formation in the 1940s, the Connolly Association had conducted a long-term campaign to unionise Irish workers.[13] Later, the 'no politics' stance stemmed from the fear of the fall-out from the IRA's military campaign in Northern Ireland and in Britain. This left a plethora of small British-based organisations in the

London area, amongst them, Troops Out, the Women and Ireland groups and the Armagh Group, Sinn Fein (Britain), the Wolfe Tone Society, as well as the Irish in Britain Representation Group (IBRG), Labour and Ireland,[14] and the National Council of Civil Liberties (now Liberty), to spearhead the struggle against the PTA in their place of work, in their trade union, their women's group, etc.

This, then, was the political environment in which pro-choice activists set to work in Britain from the beginning of the 1980s. Given that the tensions of war pervaded all types of political activity, there was considerable pressure to put what were seen as 'first things first', whether the fate of prisoners in British and Irish jails, or the plight of those 'lifted' under the PTA. Issues like reproductive rights and gay and lesbian rights were frequently judged too peripheral and best sorted out 'after the revolution'. Further, the hold of the Catholic Church on many Irish community organisations mean that these issues were not only unacceptable, but morally explosive and 'no go' areas where socially conservative organisations were concerned, regardless of the political climate.

Blazing new trails: the strange mish-mash of female London-Irish life

The vibrant job market in London, as well as training and career possibilities, such as nursing, were the main draw for women immigrants in the aftermath of the Second World War. However, as Muirin O'Briain has identified in her study of the London Irish conducted in the 1970s, there has existed a category amongst these female emigrants whose motives for leaving Ireland were not merely economic, but were fired by a sense of adventure or getting 'out of a rut.' She found that four times as many women as men surveyed emigrated for these reasons, and concluded that this was a reflection of women's relatively lower status in Irish society, poor marriage prospects and a sense of isolation in rural areas.[15] Kevin O'Connor, in his book *The Irish in Britain*, recounts that a twenty-three year old woman from a provincial city in Ireland confided: 'I had to get out, or bust. I couldn't take the heavy moral "respectability"; to be frank, I couldn't express myself sexually.'[16]

Such sentiments were expressed in spite of the best efforts of the clergy, and of the southern state's first *Taoiseach* (Prime Minister), Eamon de Valera, to depict urban living overseas as unsuited to young Irishwomen. It was argued that in fleeing from 'the green fields of Ireland [for] the grey streets of an alien underworld' they 'risked plunging into the sinks of iniquity and exchanging the spotless purity of their Irish home for the pagan turpitude of a modern Babylon'.[17] Sabina Sharkey was later to identify these alleged subversives who preferred the 'kitchens, factories and dancehalls of other lands' as 'gender dissidents'.[18] In an essay 'Sexuality for Export' which appeared in the first account of Irish lesbians and gay men, *Out for Ourselves* published in 1986, the author recounts how lesbians upped and left the homophobia of Ireland of the time, and how some found work with London Transport, a path already well-trodden by Irish women. She recalls these clippies (conductresses) 'wearing pink triangles and waving to each other as their respective buses hit the Kilburn High Road.' Through a feminist network more contacts were made with:

> ...the clippies, the community workers, the nurses and the academics – a strange mish-mash of Irish life, north and south. There were those who might be considered 'deviant', 'freak', 'unnatural' or 'mad', with untold stories of separation, divorce, adoption, abortion and of course lesbianism. There were too many lesbians in one place not to assume that we were all here for the good of our health.[19]

Cherry Smith, the journalist and poet, also speaks eloquently of her rush to embrace the liberal and progressive atmosphere of London, a place that seemed to be more or less a city state and culturally distinct from other parts of Britain. In her account of being a Northern Irish ('post-Prod Nationalist') lesbian who emigrated in 1982, she highlights the freedoms of adulthood, the opportunities to express herself in ways she had only dreamed of, that London provided. The humour, the connectedness of home, she missed, to be sure. However, these were compensated for 'by the escape from hypocrisy and provincialism of the small towns many of us came from.' The anonymity, the lack of predetermination, 'the fact that no one knows what my father does, and that no one ever suggests that I ought to be married at my age', were a great source of pleasure. She thrived on London's multiculturalism, the arts, the food, the colours of the fruit and veg stalls and of peoples' clothes witnessed just by walking to the shops. For her, she says, there was 'a family of lovers, ex-lovers and friends, which gives me the support and validation necessary to live'. In time, of course, she ran into the inevitable crux of whether to be Irish or 'to sound English, to lie low':

> I am in a gay bar and a woman asks me to dance. 'Where are you from?' she asks. 'Ireland', I reply. 'So you're a Paddy then?' I turn swiftly then and walk away as though she has slapped my mouth.[20]

Another Irish lesbian recounts how she also faced the inevitable:

> You're not really Irish are you? You don't come across like one (English feminist); You can't really be a Mick [a pejorative term, like 'Paddy'] . You must be one of the more educated ones (policeman father of a friend over the Sunday roast); I mean, I don't really think Irish people are stupid. I just wish they'd stop acting like they were (colleague at work); Look, you Bog Arab (lover in ignorance).[21]

Ide O'Carroll, a lesbian writer and academic, continues the sorry tale in an account of her arrival in London in 1993 after years spent in America. Working as a temp by day and doing her research by night, she says she encountered racism for the first time. Being Irish was always seen as desirable in the US, she says, but 'in Britain I was exposed to people who stereotyped the Irish as either 'stupid' or 'terrorists'. It was a terrible time, softened only by the love and support of a handful of Irish lesbians and gay friends.[22]

The lifestyle that Cherry Smith and so many others craved was light years away from the traditional London-Irish community organisations and recreational activities expanded and developed to meet the needs of the large 1950s influx of immigrants. These included the County Associations and 'the ballrooms of romance', like the Hibernian in Fulham, the National in Kilburn, the Garryowen in Cricklewood and the Shamrock at Elephant and Castle. The Irish dance venues were where many an amorous encounter took place, and the work-a-day world was forgotten while dancing to the strains of the big bands.

Not for women like Cherry were the dance halls or the overwhelmingly male preserves of the traditional Irish pubs of the Kilburn High Road or the Holloway Road. The latter were the hangouts of many an exhausted building labourer whiling away his evenings and his wages, determined to lose the reality of his brutal existence in drink by dragging out the hours before returning to his inhospitable landlady and unsavoury digs. Nor, indeed, the Irish Centre in Camden Town founded in 1955 under the auspices of the Catholic hierarchy, with its governing executive committee which included clerical representatives from the dioceses of Westminster, Southwark and elsewhere in London. The Centre was located in the vicinity of Euston Station, terminus of the mail-boat from Holyhead, and purchased with the assistance of loans from the Catholic Diocese of Westminster and Arthur Guinness and Sons. It was also supported with the help of grants from the Borough of Camden.[23]

Not their cup of tea either were the exclusive plush surroundings of the Irish Club in Belgravia, founded in 1948 with the aid of a donation from the Guinness family where the 'successful' Irish disported themselves. There was to be found the 'G&T/whisky&soda/bridge-playing/golfing set' who counted in their ranks the doctors and dentists attracted by the opportunities provided by the British National Health

Service set up in 1948. Also, not to be forgotten were the big builders who patronised the Club. They had done well out of Britain's building boom in its post-war reconstruction programme in London which had taken the brunt of the German bombing, together with Birmingham and Coventry. They had moved up in the world, thanks to the plentiful male unskilled labour which they, or their sub-contractors, disbursed through an infamous system known as 'The Lump'. This cash-in-hand form of payment which avoided the need for tax and insurance, was the bugbear of the trade unions and the Connolly Association.

It is also debatable whether 'new wave' Irish feminists would have seen eye to eye with George Bernard Shaw in his rejection of an invitation to join the Club. GBS's condescending retort, famously inscribed on a postcard, read as follows:

> *I can imagine nothing less desirable than an Irish Club. Irish people in England should join English clubs, and avoid each other like the plague. If they flock together like geese they might as well never have left Ireland. They don't admire, nor even like one another. In English clubs they are always welcome. More fools the English perhaps; but the two are so foreign that they have much to learn from their association and co-operation.*[24]

It would be fair to say that new-wave immigrants and second or third-generation feminist activists might steer clear of the Irish Club, but they would *not* have belittled the very worthy work going on under the Camden Irish Centre's roof. They would have well understood the purpose served by the recreational gatherings such as *céilís* – the Irish traditional music and dance gigs – ballad sessions, bingo, and the much loved Irish Bacon and Cabbage Suppers, the social welfare services, and the Marian Employment Agency run by the Centre. Similarly, they would have been aware that the rationale of the County Associations was to help alleviate the cultural shock involved in transferring from a rural environment to an urban one. They might have pooh-poohed the Centre's description of itself as 'a social centre and home-from-home for people from any part of Ireland...who are lonely in London or want a spot of Ireland in their midst.'[25] And this was not a case of class snobbery, for there were many of working-class origin and occupation amongst this grouping. It was just that a 'home-from-home' was what they wanted to avoid at all costs.

Rightly or wrongly, it has long remained a popular belief amongst many Irish in Britain that the survival of an Irish identity has been essentially bound up with the survival of Catholicism. The off-the-cuff remark made by Anne Higgins, a second-generation Irish interviewee in *Across the Water, Irish Women's Lives in Britain*, neatly sums it up: 'the Catholic and Irish thing were completely intertwined.'[26] It has been argued by academics, such as Mary Hickman, that in the education received by Irish children in Catholic schools, religion was prioritised at the expense of Irishness.[27] Sheridan Gilley, the British academic, has gone as far as saying that the Irish community was essentially the Church's own construct, given its key role in providing the building blocks of social stability, education being a crucial element, in the period after the Great Famine.[28]

However, it needs to be borne in mind that following a pattern existing in Ireland itself before the Famine, there were high levels of non-practising baptised Catholics among the Irish in Britain. One estimate, for instance, puts the level of non-church attendance amongst baptised Irish Catholics in the last quarter of the nineteenth century in England and Wales at fifty per cent.[29] Apart from the issues of identity thrown up by those Irish who are agnostics or atheists, there is also the question of where Protestants fit in. In a study conducted by Mary Kells on Northern Irish Protestant immigrants, she notes that 'Protestants who consider themselves British first, Northern Irish second, tend to feel less desire to maintain an Irish identity and are more disposed, theoretically, at least, to integrate into British society.'[30]

Creating their own spaces

Making room for new ways of thinking and being are a difficult proposition in any society. Even more difficult is the task of inserting these new ways into the communal life of an immigrant community which has struggled against the odds to find a place for itself in an unfriendly, or even hostile environment. Many of the 'new wave' preferred to divest themselves of the burden of their history and assimilate into British society. Others wanted to be Irish, but on their own terms, a process that took place at different levels. One of the most tangible outcomes was the establishment of the London Irish Women's Centre in 1983, an organisation with a feminist ethos concerned with *both* welfare issues and women's self-empowerment. At an informal level, Irish feminists, gay and straight, made forays into Irish politics, and, as described below, into the conservative world of traditional Irish music and dance.

Against this background the comments of Joan Neary[31] are salutary. Joan came to London in 1973 and was an activist in the British Women's Liberation Movement and IWASG. Also, she worked as a paid employee in voluntary sector organisations, such as Women's Aid and Haringey Women's Employment Project. She recalls that for recreational purposes she frequented English venues, especially women's centres, clubs or halls rented for special music or dance events. She had little experience of the Irish community except for going to traditional Irish set dancing and *céilís* organised by the Irish Centre in Camden Town. She says that she has never been to any of the traditional associations, such as the County Associations, and although people might be welcoming, 'I wouldn't be at home in those kind of places because it's not who I am. There's a load of issues about going back into your own community, there are ghosts from your own past. I would hate some of the values, the ones I ran away from [in Ireland], probably. My not making forays into those areas is about my own past.' Joan remembers that she and her fellow *céilí* dancers were:

...a little crew of oddly-dressed, women-dancing-with-women, not-with-families-women who enjoyed the dancing. We didn't take much notice of what people thought, although there was the odd remark passed in the toilets. There's security and power in being in a group and our one was fairly large. I remember one time when someone said there's a fancy dress thing next Sunday and we shouldn't forget to get all dressed up. And one woman standing next to me said, 'Sure aren't we in fancy dress all the time wearing whatever – dungarees, long skirts, bohemian looking outfits.' I though, well that's about right.

Joan suggests that if she and the women she describes had a relationship, however tenuous, with the Irish community in London, then they are at best located on the margins, perhaps even constituting an underground, and certainly an alternative. 'We were our bit of the Irish community', she says.

Joanne O'Brien,[32] a documentary photographer of the Irish in Britain, a member of IWASG and an activist in the British Women's Liberation Movement, enhances the picture:

Although I wasn't an IWASG stalwart having only been active in the group in its early days, I remember being involved in various fund-raising events for the group. On one occasion I was one of those who did the booking of a hall at the Irish Centre in Camden Town. We wanted to run a céilí to raise funds for IWASG's support work, and for the work of Open Line and the Well Woman in Dublin. But when we booked the hall we didn't tell the Centre that it concerned the abortion issue.

I remember very well the moment when the Irish Centre staff realised who and what we were. We were in the small lower hall downstairs and I can see it all in my mind's eye, them standing in the doorway watching us dancing. It was a women-only event, and that in itself had got them very worried. The women's Irish traditional music band, the Sheelaghs, were playing and it was a great night actually, but I was highly amused by the fact that they were shocked. It certainly seemed to raise the question of what was Irish and what wasn't, let alone the business of what was, or was not, socially acceptable.

As I recall, I don't think the women dancers were being particularly demonstrative in the way of necking or anything like that. It really was just a lot of women, gay and straight, who were mainly wearing dungarees. You know how these were de rigeur among feminists at the time. Anyone wearing a skirt had, to all intents and purposes, no political credibility whatsoever! But the idea of women doing céilí with women – and in dungarees – clearly came as a major cultural shock to the Centre people.

Marian Larragy,[33] who got involved with IWASG around 1981, makes an interesting observation about different perceptions of what a *céilí* might represent, not from the standpoint of traditional Irish organisations in Britain, or from British-based Irish feminists, but from feminists in Ireland itself. Her comments make a case for considering the varied and fluid notions of *Irishness* that can emerge at different moments in history, and in different geographical locations. Marian's comments also show how the moral climate at the London Irish Centres had changed by the mid-1990s:

One year for International Women's Day we decided to organise an event with the London Irish Women's Centre, Sólás Anois (this translates as 'consolation now' and was also meant as a pun on the English word, 'solace'), the domestic violence project, Positively Irish Action on Aids, IWASG, and others at the Camden Irish Centre. We had performances of modern and traditional material, with actors, traditional musicians, and singers, finishing with a women's céilí for a few hundred people. It was fabulous. However, some feminists over from Dublin told me that they would under no circumstances go to a 'fecking céilí' in London, and that there could be no such thing as a lesbian céilí. The whole thing, they said, was too ridiculous for words.

None of these things were enough to stop us from having several successful Irish Lesbian and Gay céilís at the Camden and Hammersmith Irish Centres. They drew people from all nationalities, religious and racial backgrounds and were especially popular with mixed race LGBT (lesbian and gay, bisexual and trans-gender) couples and friendship groups. I was once accused by a fellow volunteer at an English LGBT group of never doing anything nearly so much fun for that organisation. The simple answer was that something like that only grows out of a long period of people struggling to make things different.

Marian also relates how the position of the Federation of Irish Societies on homosexuality had progressed over the years:

In the mid-1990s I joined an Irish Lesbian and Gay group that had started in West London – we decided to call it Amach Linn!('Out with Us!'). It was a non-funded group which had been set up to advance the social and cultural welfare of Irish lesbians and gay men in London. The group met at the Hammersmith Irish Centre for around three years – till about 1997. The Centre has an Irish Welfare Advice Service. Some of the staff were involved with the group and the Centre manager was supportive. The Mayor of Hammersmith and Fulham came to some event we ran. She is second-generation Irish and was absolutely determined the Irish community organisations would observe inclusive practices. She was also keen that the Council would not relinquish control of the Centre [the Council was one of the main funders of the Hammersmith Centre until about 2008 when the Irish government through the Dion committee stepped in with funding].

The Federation of Irish Societies was also very keen that we should sign up and be seen to be affiliated. We had the impression that we were to be a badge of proof of a more progressive Federation. One of the paid officers talked movingly at our AGM about growing up gay in a Europe where that could spell death in a concentration camp. It seemed that a shift had taken place. It was not openly discussed in Irish publications here, but there were a lot of LGBT individuals working in Irish welfare organisations and the betting was that no one would openly complain about LGBT people being included in things Irish. The changes resulting from the hard-won Law Reform Act in the Republic, which abolished all previous laws criminalizing homosexual acts between men and made the age of consent the same for gays and heterosexuals, provided a sort of bona fides for the Irishness of LGBT Irish people in England.

In summary, the *alternative* Irish scene in London provided many with another type of abode, a place where they could belong which was not a 'home from home', so to speak. The Catholic ethos of traditional Irish organisations, with its opposition to birth control, to divorce and to homosexuality, and in particular to abortion, rendered these a 'no go' area for many of the younger, more secular generation at the onset of the 1980s. Jeanne Rathbone[34] of the Wandsworth Irish Women's Group, the South London Irish Women's Group and Irish Women's Perspectives, organisations active from the mid-1980s to the early 1990s, makes her feelings on the situation quite clear:

We were of that generation of women that didn't fit into the Irish Catholic (or evangelical Protestant) mould; we were modern Irish women finding our way. When I came over to London in the 1960s I felt that there was no place in the Irish community for women like me. I didn't want to go to Irish pubs. Neither did I feel comfortable in the Irish dance halls. In fact, for a number of years after I first came over here I was very isolated from the Irish community and anyone in it except for one of my sisters who lived here.

I am pro-choice, so you can imagine how difficult it would be to function in traditional Irish community groups at the time. Really, they were not the place for women like me. I was always concerned about the amount of clerical influence in these organisations. It was often very spooky for women of my generation with strong views to be going to Irish community meetings and conferences put on by them, only to find a nun or priest in mufti running the show!

I was politically aware and active quite early on. I joined the Labour Party in 1969 and didn't find a home there either, since being middle-class was iffy. The party's emphasis on the British working class, particularly the male working-class trade unionist, resulted in two fundamental aspects of my identity – being a woman and being Irish – going unrecognised. The worst thing was that I went along with it and was assimilated into that way of thinking for years.

I felt – and still feel – that we, Irish feminists, have a lot to celebrate. When people think of Irish women it's often the doom and gloom over the lack of reproductive rights. I was once asked to speak at the launch of a book on sexuality by Shere Hite[35] and was directed to discuss abortion and contraception in the Irish context, something I really resented. She [Hite] had decided that our lack of these rights were what summed us [Irish women] up. But on the reproductive rights front, Irish feminists' struggles here and at home have been heroic. This is so easy to forget. Also we should remember all the positives. Irish female emigrants have a unique history: the fact that there are more of us than men, that many of us emigrated as single women, that we forged our own way here; that many of us got an education and climbed the career ladder.

There's also the fact that considerable numbers of us (myself included) who married non-Irish men, straddled two cultures and tried to inculcate in our children a sense of their Irish heritage, often against all the odds. In my own case, I made the decision to become a school governor at my children's school for eighteen years. I also got involved with the Inner London Education Authority

(ILEA) to challenge its failure to recognise that the Irish are the largest immigrant group, and that they suffer from discrimination, prejudice and disadvantage, and that their culture and history are excluded from the curriculum.

It wasn't until the early 80s, with the impetus from the GLC initiatives, that the women's and Irish dimension came together for us. We didn't feel isolated – visibility at last! There seemed to be Irish feminists involved in all sorts of political and artistic activities. I was convenor of Battersea Labour Party's Women's Section. We had adopted Charlotte Despard, who had stood as the Labour candidate in 1918. Her biography was subtitled 'Socialist, Suffragette and Sinn Feiner'[36] – the latter referred to her activities in supporting Irish independence and relocating to Ireland to help her friend, Maud Gonne McBride.

I then became a paid feminist when I got a job as Women's Officer in Hammersmith and Fulham Council. I went on to tutor 'Taste of Ireland' courses in adult education and became a trainer for 'Irish People and Equal Opportunities' working for local authorities and voluntary organisations. With this renewed confidence in my identity as an Irishwoman, I went into comedy with a one woman show working under the name SHEELA-NA-GIG. Sheela (an ancient female, masturbating stone carving found on cornerstones on castles and churches all over Ireland – an assault on male conceit and prudery) makes a suitable role model for menopausal, pagan Irish women compared to, say, the Virgin Mary, the Mother of Sorrows. When I performed at the Edinburgh Festival in 1995 I was compared to Dave Allen, one of Ireland's best known sophisticated, satirical comedians.

Now, in the last phase of my meandering career, I am a Humanist Celebrant, the ideal job for a practising atheist. I conduct namings, weddings and funerals and I had the privilege of taking Dave Allen's funeral service. I guess there wouldn't be enough demand for my services back home in Galway yet, though the-times-they-are-a-changing.

As if to bear out the point made by Jeanne Rathbone about the Catholic ethos of many London-Irish organisations, several interviewees who were either employed by Irish organisations or volunteered in them, have commented on the extent of opposition to progressive ideas on women's rights or gay rights until the middle to late 1990s, although the position on abortion has not shifted to date. One interviewee who wishes to remain anonymous, points out some of the malicious remarks that were made about the London Irish Women's Centre and its counselling service:

I worked for an Irish organisation throughout the 1980s and 90s. I was aware of the comments going around in the world of Irish welfare and support services regarding the London Irish Women's Centre (LIWC), for instance. In particular, I used to hear that the counselling service there was only for women who were lesbians or who wanted an abortion.

In fact, it was quite commonly stated that you went to LIWC to be put 'in the right direction' by counsellors there. This flew in the face of the professional practice of confidential, non-judgemental, and non-directive counselling. All of the counsellors at LIWC would have stood by these principles. If women asked for information and were given it, then it was up to the individual client to do what she wanted with it. If a counsellor behaves professionally she will not direct any woman to have, or not have, an abortion. It's people's own decision to do what they want with their bodies.[37]

While the negative labelling of feminists as peddlers of abortion and lesbianism did the rounds in London-Irish circles, Brid Boland, a founder member of the London Irish Women's Centre, says that the Centre 'had to pressure the *Irish Post* to print the word *abortion* in the early days [the Centre was founded in 1983] and also the word *lesbian*, thus earning ourselves the brand of extreme radicalism amongst Irish community organisations and individuals.'[38] the *Irish Post's* lack of enthusiasm in printing the 'unmentionable' was highlighted at a workshop run by the Irish Lesbian Group at the third London Irish Women's Conference in 1987 hosted by the LIWC. In their report of the conference, the LIWC argued that 'many [Irish lesbians] were forced to shed their Irish identity and assimilate into English society to find support in the English Feminist Movement.'[39] The steps forward made as the 1990s progressed have never included IWASG or Iasc; neither of these organisation were ever called in from 'the cold'.

Multiculturalism, the Irish community and the fallout on Irish feminism in Britain

The question may well be asked how Irish organisations, many of them the recipients of funding from British bodies, often the local state, were able to pursue exclusive practices when it came to assessing the needs of Irish immigrants in Britain. Many of these British bodies have proudly upheld an equal rights policy including a 'woman's right to choose'. This question may not have been posed very frequently in the Irish context, but it has been one much mulled over by disadvantaged sectors of other ethnic groupings, particularly by women, gays and young people. The conclusion invariably reached is that the root of the problem lies in the British state's (at national and local level) policy of multiculturalism, one which more or less allowed ethnic groups to monitor and police themselves in what were deemed 'private' and 'family' matters.

Until the British state declared it dead in the water in the aftermath of the 7/7 London bombings,[40] the policy of multiculturalism underpinned the funding of ethnic minority groups. The concept, said to have originated in Canada in response to tensions between its English and French-speaking populations, has a history in Britain stretching back to the mid-1960s. Its stated aim of 'equal opportunity accompanied by cultural diversity, in an atmosphere of mutual tolerance', was set out by the Labour Home Secretary Roy Jenkins in 1966.[41] It was employed as a strategy by the state in its attempt to 'deal with' the absorption of non-white minorities already settled in Britain, while at the same time as introducing rigid immigration controls, notably through the first Race Relations Act (1965) and the Local Government Act (1966). It was a strategy diametrically opposed to the assimilation policies of the French state.

Multiculturalism – the pros and cons

Multiculturalism challenged the notion of a single, definable and standardised (British) culture by giving weight to an ethic of 'equal opportunity, accompanied by cultural diversity', in one of the most multicultural and racially mixed societies in the world. Its positive achievement was that it allowed different communities to be acknowledged and valued with new, official respect. Translated into education, for instance, teaching about the various religious holidays, whether Hindu, Islamic, Sikh, Jewish or Christian, was seen as one way of acquainting children with cultures other than their own. History teaching began to include coverage of issues, like the effects of slavery and the Irish Great Famine. As Jeanne Rathbone says above: 'Visibility at last!'

At local government level, funding for projects devoted to establishing equal opportunity for minorities came into being, beginning in earnest when the left-wing Greater London Council (GLC) took up office in County Hall, following its success in the elections of 1981. Other metropolitan councils soon followed suit. It was from that time that Irish organisations in London began to receive local government funding, whether from the GLC directly or from local borough councils. In response to the vigorous campaigning of many activists, Ken Livingstone, leader of the GLC, supported by his second-generation Irish Deputy, John McDonnell, backed the recognition of the Irish as an ethnic minority, eligible for funding of welfare and cultural projects under the policy of multiculturalism. This was on the basis that the Irish experienced discrimination, especially in the areas of housing, employment, education and stereotyping in the media, all of which were outlined in the Policy Report on the Irish Community produced by the GLC's strategic Policy Unit in 1984. An Irish Liaison Officer was appointed by the GLC in 1983. This resulted in a consultation conference being held to decide on the shape and form of policies and activities of the Irish in London. Within the short span of a couple of years there were approximately thirty Irish voluntary sector (NGO-type) funded welfare and cultural services set up in the capital.[42]

Critics have long argued that a multicultural celebration of diversity gave rise to what became known as the 'saris, samosas, and steel-bands syndrome'. This implied that although welfare issues were being addressed there was undue concentration on external expressions of difference, like clothing, food, and music. In the Irish case, these differences were demonstrated through, for instance, the annual St. Patrick's Day Parade, for which its organisers have received funds from the Greater London Authority (GLA). At this level, it was said that the policy of multiculturalism failed to tackle the racism buried deep in the power structures in British society at large. If anything, it caused ethnic groups to be separated into distinct blocks delineated by culture (increasingly associated with religion – Hindu, Sikh, Muslim, Catholic, Jewish, etc.) rather than race, thereby segmenting and dividing communities from each other.

It was said that where the growth of identity politics was encouraged, it led to separatism, 'parallel lives', the entrenching of religious conservatism, even fundamentalism, and the fostering of unelected 'community leaders', frequently male. In the words of Yasmin Ali, an academic writing on Muslim women in the North of England, 'through multiculturalism the state sought to find a means whereby the "integration" of South Asian communities could be achieved by constructing a stratum of mediators who could represent the community to the state (usually the local state) and interpret that state to the community, without recourse to the ballot box...'[43]

One of the critics of multiculturalism, Arun Kundnani, deputy editor of the journal *Race and Class* at the London-based Institute of Race Relations, suggests that when funding became available, the policy of multiculturalism made for the creation of a 'race relations industry'. He argues that 'the fight against racism came to be redefined as a fight for ethnic recognition, as if funding an ethnic project, any ethnic project no matter how dubious, was to tackle racism.'[44] The policy of multiculturalism allowed for the monitoring and self-policing of different ethnic groups conducted by 'race managers', 'race relations officers', 'ethnic entrepreneurs', but more often than not, those known as 'community leaders' who were nearly always male. These were points consistently made by other critics, such as Southall Black Sisters based in the West London borough of Ealing.[45]

The impact of self-policing meant that hierarchies and power structures *within* the ethnic groups the policy was designed to serve were not tackled. Numerous instances have been recorded of gross abuses of power in ethnic groups by 'community leaders' in cases of domestic violence, forced marriages, and even the murder of women and children. The police, for their part, invoked 'respect' for cultural and religious differences as a reason for passing up interfering in the 'private' arena of the family.[46]

In Irish community circles, many issues, not least abortion, homosexuality, HIV/Aids, sexual abuse, and domestic violence, were more than likely to have been kept within the 'family', or preferably, swept under the carpet were it not for the setting up in the early 1980s through to the middle 1990s of an array of radical groups to force these issues. Some of the groups functioned on an entirely voluntary basis, like IWASG and Iasc, *Amach Linn*! and the Irish Lesbian Group. Others received funding, examples being the London Irish Women's Centre, Action Group for Irish Youth, the domestic violence support service, *Sólás Anois*, and Positively Irish Action Group on Aids, the latter being a support service for Irish people affected by HIV/Aids.

As stated earlier, considerable funding has come from British organisations. Primarily, these are either local government institutions or charitable bodies, such as the

National Lottery Charities Board and the City Parochial Foundation. However, two Irish benefactors entered the arena in the 1980s, one being the Ireland Fund of Great Britain, and Dion, the Irish Government's Advisory Committee for the Irish Community in Britain, which is administered by the Irish Embassy in London. Its function is to disburse funds provided by the government of the Republic to Irish immigrant welfare agencies in Britain as a whole. In consequence, funded organisations may well have had to take account of the policies of the Irish state in a manner not required by the British state under its remit of multiculturalism, the abortion issue being a prime example. It goes without saying, that had IWASG sought funding from Dion on the grounds that the group's abortion support service was being provided to meet the welfare needs of residents of the Republic, the response was hardly likely to have been a positive one, given Irish government policy on the abortion issue to date.

The question of how influential Irish government funding is in the policy making of community organisations in Britain remains unanswered, if the responses received while putting this book together are anything to go by. The stock answer to informal requests by this author for clarification of their stance on the abortion issue, including to leading members of the Federation of Irish Societies, was invariably, 'abortion isn't an issue for us/it just doesn't come up/it isn't on our agenda anyway'. Does this mean that organisations like the Federation are well aware of the trail of abortion seekers across the Irish Sea, but are swayed by the fear of losing Dion's financial support, however small this contribution may be to their overall funds? Alternatively, does it mean that the 'Catholic ethos' is so deeply ingrained that the issue of abortion seekers is automatically edited out? What does this mean when it comes to needs assessments of the welfare of Irish women, however transient they may be? What does it mean for those undertaking their support on British soil?

Many Asian and African feminist groups up and down Britain, like Southall Black Sisters, have long challenged their communities on issues hidden in the private domain of the family, especially domestic violence, forced marriage, and female circumcision. In the process, they have earned for themselves the accolade 'homebreakers' and 'harlots'. When asked, IWASG members invariably answered that they were not willing to run the gauntlet where Irish community organisations were concerned. When asked why they felt unable or unwilling to challenge the status quo, some members insisted that it would involve 'a struggle too many' and 'a struggle too far'; in sum, a fight on all fronts. Several said they cringed at the thought of an endless round of meetings and the boundless energy they would have to invest in such an endeavour, all of which was likely to come to nought 'in the heel of the hunt'. All of the women concerned were in full-time jobs, several had young children, and many had elderly, and sometimes very needy parents, mostly living in Ireland. As 'dutiful daughters' they regularly wended their way across the Irish Sea by the ferry until cheap flights made such journeys quick and easy.

Angie Birtill gave an example of what would be involved in tackling the issue of abortion with Irish community organisations when she described an intervention made by the London Irish Women's Centre after it was found that counsellors, one of whom was a nun, at the domestic violence project, *Sólás Anois*, were unwilling to entertain, let alone discuss the issue with pregnant clients, some of whom were likely to have experienced brutal rape. On arrival at the meeting, she and a committee member of LIWC were met with a room filled with the serried ranks of representatives of London-Irish organisations. Needless to say, Angie and her colleague were left under no illusion that they were outnumber and outgunned.

On the issue of secrecy, some IWASG women said there was the worry that speaking out might do more harm than good, especially in Ireland. For others, there was also the problem of anti-Irish racism, most particularly for the duration of 'the Troubles'. This position was based on the belief that Irish organisations would be attacked in the media for their 'backwardness' and unwillingness to meet the needs of their own people, especially of 'their women'. Needless to say, racism has also been problematic for many other ethnic minority women who have been lulled into believing that they should subordinate their grievances to the 'greater good' of their communities.

Apart from racism, those interviewed spoke of an aversion, a sense of déjà vu even, to tackling a problem they had run away from in Ireland. This related to what they see as the strength of feeling and deep-seated attachment of many Irish immigrants to Catholic beliefs, prevalent even amongst ex-Catholics, although all agreed that as an ideology conservative Catholicism is not alone in its opposition to abortion. Asked to comment on the subject, the anonymous interviewee with almost two decades' experience in Irish community work, suggests how difficult engaging in protracted hostilities might be, with this stern and uncompromising reminder:

Over here [in England], the church and the Irish government have historically worked in cahoots. Even though there may be few clerics present at the decision-making tables these days, the church still has a tremendous influence on Irish immigrants and their children where certain issues are concerned, for instance, on homosexuality and abortion. Despite the recent dwindling numbers in their congregations, the church still has a great deal of power. People may not be regular church-goers, but they are baptised, married and buried within the church, and they send their children to Catholic schools. Don't be surprised to see that influence reflected on the various committees, not least at the Dion committee meetings held at the Irish Embassy in London, and usually chaired by the First or Third Secretaries. No rocking of the boat there, you can be sure![47]

Céilí following 1987 London Irish Women's Centre Conference
© Joanne O'Brien

IWASG picket of Camden Irish Centre on the occasion of
Gemma Hussey's attendance at a St. Patrick's Day dinner in 1983
© Joanne O'Brien

CHAPTER 4

Beginnings and Bloodlines: the first phase of the Irish Women's Abortion Support Group (IWASG)

She came to stay[1]

*F*rom the start, she wasn't like the others. Alright, so she was a bit like a few of the others who had made it to Heathrow (or Gatwick, or Luton, or Stansted), but at the last lap stood rooted to the spot unable to move. It was about eleven when she phoned. She sounded panic stricken and blurted out in a little-girl voice, 'I'm here!' I said, 'Right!', knowing instinctively who she was. Somewhat annoyed, though, I thought, 'Oh, God, you're a Belfast city girl. Surely you can make the last few hundred yards to the Tube on your own?' We had talked through the directions on the phone the night before, and she was word perfect.

She stood stiff and immobile at the Information Desk, looking as if she hadn't moved since we spoke. Taking in that she was in shock, I mouthed the usual inane pleasantries: 'Hallo, I'm Ann. So you made it, then. Do you fancy a cup of tea/coffee before we head off?' What struck me was how incongruous she looked: a Barbie doll of a young woman made up to the nines. She was a platinum blond with a Charlie's Angels hairdo – you know, the one Farrah Fawcett had made all the rage once upon a time in the 80s – and tight black Lycra top and pants. She looked like a woman well able to find her way around, but not this time round it seemed...

At the clinic that afternoon she made it through the pre-op medical routines. Her blood and other tests done and dusted, she got herself signed and certified to say she qualified for an abortion under the 1967 Act. The only glitch was when she appeared grim and strained coming out of a much longer than usual counselling session. I wondered what she had said in there. Had she spoken of her fears, whatever they were? All I could bring myself to say was, 'Are we done?', and she acquiesced. I burbled a few comments about us going home and getting the dinner going, and continued with whatever nervous chitchat one engages in to disguise troubled situations.

The night was disturbed by a seemingly endless series of telephone calls and fraught conversations, often very loud. We, the host family, sat in the kitchen thinking it unwise to take to our beds, only to be pitched out of them once the noise started up again. Angry at what was happening, I picked up the phone at one stage and caught the ravings of a drunken voice at the other end accusing me of murdering his child. 'I'll get the RUC on you if you don't get off my phone,' I shouted, something which, given my political convictions, I never thought I'd hear myself utter for the duration of 'the Troubles' . 'Don't you know they've all the phones tapped in the North', I added for good measure, without knowing if that applied to private lines, and not just to public pay phones. The line went dead.

At six in the morning, after a few hours' sleep, I was awakened as a head appeared round the bedroom door, asking, 'Where do you keep the hairdryer?'. It was hard to know what to make of such a request in the early hours. I was knackered, but all the same I dragged myself up and furnished her with the required item. She was already washed, dressed and kitted out with enough war paint for a night on the town, including a liberal application of fluorescent blue eyeshadow. 'Chances are they'll have to wash all that off before you go to theatre today, seeing you're having a full anaesthetic', I said to her somewhat peevishly, suffering from a version of ' the morning after the night before' syndrome. She seemed unperturbed and said, 'It's what I face the world with; it's my armour, you know.' And, as a kind of afterthought, she added, 'Sorry about last night, that was my brother on the phone. He can be such a pain when he's drunk.'

One can only hazard a guess at the extent of the negative mental health effects, and even physical damage, induced by this woman's pregnancy in an incestuous relationship, given prevailing taboos. Although she felt that over the years she had been privy to the full gamut of abortion experiences, the incident also left its mark on the IWASG member supporting the woman. This stemmed not only from a humanitarian point of view, but also from frustration at the political realities (or unrealities) involved. Plainly, this was a troubled situation crying out for the help and support of professionals on the woman's home turf. Even more plain was the fact that the IWASG woman was way out of her depth!

The emergence of IWASG as a humanitarian and political project

Needless to say, not many abortion seekers who came into the lives of IWASG members did so in such extraordinary circumstances. Nonetheless, each woman's experience has proved difficult and traumatic in some way or another. It was in recognition of such a state of affairs that IWASG was formed in the early 1980s. Abortion seekers frequently found themselves in straitened financial circumstances after raising money for clinic fees and travel. Consequently, they depended on being put up by relatives, friends, and friends of friends before the overnight residency requirement was removed in 2001.[2]

In essence, IWASG's formation was based on a long-standing tradition of Irish women, and sometimes men, whether living in Ireland or Britain, helping out in difficult circumstances. Anecdotal evidence suggests that long before the 1967 Abortion Act came into place, such help was also given to those trying to access whatever illegal services were available in Britain, whether back street or Harley Street. Ellen Mullin,[3] a Dubliner who came to London in 1978, was one such. She was never a member of the support group but recalls helping three women while living and working in London. Ellen ascribes her empathy with the plight of the women she encountered as stemming from her own background and life experiences. She explains:

I grew up in a very conservative Co. Dublin household. I had a private education and the role of women was one in which you were expected to cultivate a very wonderful appearance, and you had to have a good academic record in order to be able to attract 'Mr. Right'. And, I'm afraid, I rebelled against all of that. When I was working in Dublin I used to go to what was practically an underground family planning clinic. This clinic was in Leeson Street, and a doctor and two nurses used to come each week from somewhere in the UK. One had to phone what was practically a secret number to get an appointment. There was a fee for the appointment and the contraceptives had to be paid for separately. Patients had a physical examination, and the doctor decided which brand of the contraceptive pill was suitable. The pill had to be purchased there on the premises, and not at a pharmacy.

I was teaching at the time and my net salary was 125 punt a month, and a three-month supply of oral contraceptives was 65 punt, an awful lot of money for me. However, I had decided that I wasn't going to be sexually active without taking precautions. So rare were contraceptives in those days that friends would often ask me if they could have a look at them, like I had a novelty pack of sweets. At the time, contraceptives were prohibited by law in the Republic. Doctors did get around that by prescribing them as 'cycle regulators', but usually to married women only, which explains why it took a visiting UK doctor to prescribe to unmarried women like me.

About 38,000 women in the Republic were known to be on 'cycle regulators' in the mid-1970s.[4] Legislative change did not occur until 1979 when contraception was legalised, but for married couples only. It would take another six years for the Irish government to legalise contraception for all those over the age of eighteen, married or single. Unlike most single women of the time, Ellen Mullin was not prepared to buckle down and do. It took a brave woman to challenge the status quo, and to be sufficiently innovative in finding a solution to her contraceptive needs. It also took someone very plucky to be willing to break the law, to face the legal consequences, and her family's condemnation, if she were found out. Regarding her family, Ellen says she was so oppositional at that stage in her life that parental disapproval was not something that worried her unduly!

Ellen was well aware of the tragedy which could befall women if they became pregnant – the guilt, the loneliness, the lack of money, the fear and anxiety. Like so many Irish people, she is horrified at the recent exposure of the fate of 'fallen' women incarcerated in the Convent Magdalen Asylums well into the 1970s, and that it took until the 1990s for the last of these to close.[5] Slowly, but surely Irish people are coming to terms with this grim episode in their history where inmates washed their 'sin' – and their lives away – in the laundries of the religious orders. Among those now 'washing their dirty linen in public', saying things that had never been said before, was the late Nuala O'Faolain in her hugely popular memoir, *Are You Somebody?*[6] published in 1996.

As a result of speaking candidly of lust and sexual experience, gay and straight, and the consequences, O'Faolain's many readers wrote to her to say how much they empathised with her depiction of sexual encounters in her student and odd-job days in late 1950s. In O'Faolain's case, this was set in a Dublin that was contraceptive-free, relieved only by drinking, talking and intensive cinema-going as a means of sublimating passion. Her readers laughed wryly at her graphic recounting of gropings behind dance halls and cinemas, from which she emerged the worst for wear with sore lips and swollen breasts. And, they, like her, were hard put to make sense of a culture, at once obsessed with sex, but intent on turning its repression into a national project then, and even now.

Ellen Mullin recounts the first time she lent a hand to a woman in a 'spot of trouble', as it was known:

My first experience of helping a woman who had found herself pregnant was actually taking her to a clinic to find out if she was pregnant or not. We were both Irish living in London, and we worked at the same office. We told colleagues we were nipping out for a coffee rather than going for a pregnancy test at a family planning clinic. We worked for a social services department, and although we shared the same nationality we had very different experiences of being Irish. In consequence, the process of her revealing to me that she thought she was pregnant, that she was vulnerable, and that she needed help, probably took some guts on her part.

So, as we sat on these hard chairs waiting for the results of her pregnancy test, a buzzer sounded – this was the signal to the reception staff that the client's test was positive. Oh my God, I thought, what are we going to do? She went as white as a sheet. I wasn't really sure about how to offer her any reassurance or support, but we had to deal with the process of her acknowledging that she was pregnant.

We walked back to the office and I told her that I would keep this information confidential and that I would do anything I could to help her with whatever decision she made. She was in the middle of planning her wedding; it was going to take place in a rural area of Ireland with her traditional Catholic family very much involved. Her wedding dress was being made and she had had fittings for it. Altering it to fit a growing waistline was something she couldn't even contemplate. Walking down the aisle 'showing' was inconceivable! She said she would go to her boyfriend and think about it.

It was then decided that she was going to have an abortion. So we made arrangements for her to go to a clinic in Richmond. She and her boyfriend had very little money. I still remember getting up really early one very nippy morning and cycling to the cash point at the National Westminster Bank in Hammersmith where my salary used to get paid in. I had to withdraw what I believe was £130. Her boyfriend pulled up in a truck – he was a builder – and I handed it to him.

The boyfriend was very shy, very embarrassed about me giving him the money, about his girlfriend being pregnant, etc. I said, 'Look, just have it.' He said, 'We'll pay it back, we'll give you the interest'. I said, 'Never mind all that, just look after her'. After all these years I can still see myself standing at that cash point. I can still see the look on that young man's face.

Legal but not above board

From the beginning, IWASG's work took on the aura of the underground. Confidentiality was of paramount importance where abortion seekers were concerned. As well as the need for confidentiality, there was hostility from the majority of London-Irish organisations, which meant that the group's activities never became headline news in the *Irish Post* or the *Irish World*. In effect, abortion might have been legal in Britain, but in London-Irish circles it was far from being above board. A further complication was that many IWASG members were reluctant to divulge the nature of their work for fear of distressing their own families. Writing in the British journal, *Feminist Review*, group members spoke of the contradictions involved:

We are conditioned as women to be helpful, to look after other people, but there seems to be a contradiction in providing support for women having abortions, as it would never be seen as a good cause... It is a subversive activity – enabling women to have terminations undermines the dominant values of both the Church and State in Ireland.[7]

If abortion was below ground in traditional Irish circles, this was less the case generally in Britain in the 1980s when IWASG and Escort,[8] its sister organisation in Liverpool, got underway. As early as 1936, Stella Browne, one of the co-founders of the British Abortion Law Reform Association, had passionately declared her support for reproductive rights, because, she insisted, 'our bodies are our own'.[9] The connection between mind, body and politics ('the personal is political') was to prove central to how feminists from the late 1960s onwards came to see the importance of women deciding on their fertility, that is, the right to make choices about child-bearing and child-rearing. The pursuit of this right propelled many women into radical political activity, creating a grassroots women's health movement that grew outside the perimeters of existing political parties, such as the Labour Party, and organisations like the trade union movement, but which brought considerable influence to bear on both of these.

In 1967, the British Abortion Act which established in law that an abortion is legal in specific instances, was a pioneering piece of legislation and the result of a long history of struggle led by the Abortion Law Reform Association. The organisation had been formed in 1936 by women's rights campaigners who were joined by doctors and lawyers to fight for change in laws dating back to 1802.[10] The early nineteenth-century law punished those performing an abortion before quickening (the first time the pregnant woman feels the foetus move), but more leniently than inducing an abortion after quickening, a crime which could merit capital punishment. In 1837, the quickening clause was abolished. The 1861 Offences Against the Person Act further toughened the law to include prosecution of those, including the pregnant woman herself, attempting to induce an abortion at all stages of pregnancy which carried a maximum sentence of life imprisonment.

Unlike Ireland where infanticide was more common, backstreet abortion in Britain was widespread. Abortifacient liquids were taken, such as very hot lysol, gin, salts,

Beecham's pills, Widow Welch's pills, and various concoctions made, for instance, of herbs, ergot or slippery elm bark. Objects, such as Higginson's syringe, a rubber catheter through which a jet of fluid was directed into the cervix, or even leeches, knitting needles and coat hangers, were inserted into the uterus, thus puncturing the foetal membranes. Many women ended up with a damaged uterus, heavy blood loss and infection, or in some cases they died from the ordeal. As late as 1960 the maternal death rate in England and Wales was 31 per 100,000 live and stillbirths; in 1960 as a result of improvements in anaesthesia and antibiotics, this fell to 14 per 100,000. Eight years after the introduction of the 1967 Act, this had fallen to two per 100,000.[11]

The long road towards fertility control in Ireland

As well as being motivated to support Irish abortion seekers for humanitarian reasons, many IWASG members also had strong political reasons for doing so. Irish feminists, like their British counterparts, were concerned to separate sexual intercourse from pregnancy and motherhood, to loosen, or even destroy, the control of church, state, and the medical profession over women's lives. The feminist slogan 'Not the church, not the state, women will decide their fate' resonated with them, given their experience of their own mothers and grandmothers being subjected to recurring maternity and to confinement in the home. This condition was in conflict with the desire of many (but by no means all) of them to successfully combine motherhood with paid employment, and even a career. Marian Larragy, an IWASG member, says that her mother, who gave birth to nine children, told her once that she would have spaced them better, if she had known there was such a possibility. Sadly, she had little appreciation of the fact that the Catholic Church she adhered to has worked so hard to keep her and others from knowing that they can make choices.

In this vein, Nuala O'Faolain reflects in her memoir on her mother's end-of-life wasteland of frustrated ambition. Despite its extremes of alcoholism, despair, and the onset of mental illness, it had a ring of truth about it for the Irish women who read it in their thousands. Her mother, Nuala says, had spent much of her adult life feeding, clothing and cleaning the nine children who survived after thirteen pregnancies while coping with money problems and a lady-killer and man-about-town of a husband. In her final years, her life's work over, she just cut herself off from 'life' and sat in a chair in her Dublin flat oblivious to 'the mess', i.e. ignoring the housework (a cardinal sin in the Irish female tradition), as much as she dispensed with the role of dutiful, 'always on tap' Granny. In that bleak setting she read and drank all day, there being nothing else she wished to do.

Such a state of being seriously confounds the defining characteristics of what Aine McCarthy[12] in her study of mothers in twentieth-century Irish fiction calls the 'Good Mammy'. This archetypal and idealised mother figure of Irish (Jewish, Indian, etc.) lore, is self-sacrificing, dedicated to family and God(s), possibly in that order, and is the source of 'selfless love and good dinners'. Nuala O'Faolain's account of her aged mother's bizarre opting out touched a raw nerve in Irish society. However much critics declared it 'off the wall' and exceptional in its details, it certainly triggered many women to cast a cold eye on their own and their mother's lives on the issue of women's confinement to the home.

Mrs. O'Faolain's misfortune was to have married in the late 1930s, a time her daughter calls 'a living tomb for women', one when Irish women generally had few marketable skills, apart from domestic ones, and without hope of economic independence given the state of the nation and sky-high male unemployment. There were also statutory bars affecting married women in national (junior) school teaching, in the civil service and in state-run services generally. Such restrictions on married women's employment in the southern state were underpinned by the 1937 constitutional imperative, prompted by the *Taoiseach* of the

Republic, Eamon de Valera, which decreed that 'mothers shall not be obliged by economic necessity to engage in labour to the neglect of their duties inside the home'. Married women in Northern Ireland fared somewhat better, reflecting the fact that in certain areas, like Belfast and Derry, industrial work was available.[13]

In many respects Mrs. O'Faolain's experience was hardly exceptional compared with the women of continental Europe in the period, whether of France, Spain, Italy and elsewhere. There, conservative and reactionary regimes attempted to reduce women to their maternal role to the exclusion of others, regardless of their circumstances, such as lone parenthood and/or low income. What was exceptional, however, was the enduring high birth rate. According to various studies done on the subject,[14] fertility in the Republic was considerably higher than in any other western European country from the 1950s up to 2000, a period in history when its control gradually became the norm. Even in the 1960s, thirty per cent of all births in the Republic were fifth births or higher. This figure had reduced to fifteen per cent by 1980, and to five per cent by 1990. By 1999, the average number of children born to women in the Republic was 1.89, below the level necessary for the population to replace itself.[15]

Under the growing alignment of the Catholic Church and the new southern Irish state, formed following the War of Independence (1919-1921) and the Civil War (1922-1923), the Censorship of Publications Act of 1929 removed from the public gaze material that was seen to 'advocate the unnatural prevention of contraception or the procurement of abortion or miscarriage.' Contraceptive devices were outlawed by means of the 1935 Criminal Law Amendment Act. Adding insult to injury, the Public Dance Halls Act was also passed in 1935 requiring places used for dancing ('occasions of sin', as they were called by the clergy) be controlled and supervised. Together with the 1937 constitutional directive which ensured the enforced domesticity of mothers, the newly independent state set about creating what has been called a 'well-fenced package of legislative barriers to the advancement of the status of women in production and reproduction'.[16]

Analysis of the statistics on family size in Northern Ireland shows that large families were common amongst Catholics, particularly those defined as semi-skilled and unskilled. Although family size has been smaller amongst Protestants, a similar pattern according to occupation is discernable, with unskilled and semi-skilled working-class families having on average one or two more children than their middle class counterparts. In the population overall, the figure was four children per couple marrying in the aftermath of the Second World War, falling to 3.3 children in the early 1960s. Between 1961 and 1983 the two and three-child family became more dominant, especially since 1971.[17]

In both Irish states, it is clear that the decline in family size with the progress of the twentieth century represented the strength of feeling amongst women – and men – of the need to regulate family size for a number of reasons. Chief amongst these was the desire for a higher standard of living, greater educational expectations of children, which in turn require financial outlay, and improvements in maternal health and well-being. With the onset of feminist ideas of women's self-fulfilment and empowerment from the 1970s onwards, it would appear that the die was cast and the Catholic Church, and to a lesser degree, the Protestant churches, were being forced to concede to the modernisation of Irish society.

CHAPTER 5

The work of the Irish Women's Abortion Support Group (IWASG)

Contemporary feminism...has developed a unique system of 'self-help' networks and whereas 'self-help' is a process common to oppressed peoples, for feminism, the personal is political and 'self-help' is no less than the conscious response to women's perceived and stated needs...

Ruth Riddick[1]

The key role of British and Spanish organisations in sustaining IWASG

About the same time as IWASG was formed, a sister organisation, the Spanish Women's Abortion Support Group (SWASG), was set up. Both IWASG and SWASG emerged out of debates, often taking place collectively, where Irish and Spanish feminists in London decided to do something practical about the plight of abortion seekers from their respective countries. In the Spanish case, it was a response to the arrival of several hundred Spanish 'tourists' at London airports every week. An example of the volume of this category of 'tourist', is that in 1985 there were 17,688 abortions performed on Spanish women in Britain, a figure which reduced to 11,935 in 1986. A significant number of these were late abortions, being eighteen weeks and over. Unlike its Irish Republic counterpart, Spanish law at the time allowed abortion in cases of rape, danger to the life of the mother and severe foetal malformation.[2]

From their inception in 1981 until 1984, SWASG and IWASG operated from Release, the British drug-takers' support and advocacy agency based in London, where two paid staff members allocated a portion of their time to Irish and Spanish abortion support work. Iris Lyle,[3] a Spanish-speaking Northern Irish woman who worked for the Spanish group remembers:

The support work was on a very small scale – it was part of many other things we did in Release and I can't remember the proportion – but we really offered something useful, something very concrete. Even though I spoke Spanish it was very draining, as many of the women [abortion seekers] didn't know any English and required help with more or less everything. Those on the rota [for putting women up, escorting them to the clinic, etc.] spoke some Spanish. The Spanish women would be very upset over the great secrecy, all the scheming they had to do. They were in a terrible state. When the abortion was over it was like a great weight was lifted off them.

Iris recalls that although Release was mainly a drugs agency, providing information and advice about legal and illegal drugs, and the legal framework surrounding their use, it extended its work to include gay rights, women's rights and a whole range of issues. For example, Release was the first organisation to support the right to artificial insemination. The organisation operated as a collective and was financed through a trust fund and grants from both the Greater London Council and Urban Aid. In 1983, as a result of a dispute within Release over the reluctance of some in the organisation to continue to do abortion support work with a view to greater focus on more drug-related issues, Iris says she experienced considerable pressure. This reluctance did not stem from contradictions over the issue of abortion, she suggests, since workers, male and female alike, were strongly feminist and pro-choice, but over focus. She, together with IWASG and SWASG, lobbied Release to reverse their decision.

Iris reports that Release 'would not budge' on the issue of abortion support work and, as a result, she resigned her post. Her co-worker had already resigned and she says that some time elapsed before Release agreed to cover both Spanish and Irish abortion seekers' needs on a very limited basis. Iris travelled to Central and South America for a year where she contacted women's groups, most, if not all, actively concerned with the lack of reproductive rights and the vast problem of unsafe backstreet abortions. On her return to London she joined the Nicaragua Solidarity Campaign and continued to do abortion support work, particularly with Spanish women, but as a volunteer.

In 1984/5, following another period of political disquiet in Release over the need to curtail the range of their work, several collective members lost their jobs and abortion work was discontinued. Joan Neary recollects that there was a short gap when telephone calls were not answered and the support service ceased. However, soon after, the Irish and Spanish support groups found a new home (seen by many as the natural home) at the Women's Health and Reproductive Rights Information Centre, a British organisation which had grown out of the Women's Reproductive Rights Campaign and which was fully supportive of the work of IWASG and SWASG.

With the cumbersome acronym of WHRRIC, which few people ever got their tongues around, the organisation was ultimately located at Tindlemanor, the Women's Collective building at 52-54 Featherstone Street near Old Street Station. The Collective had received money from the Greater London Council with which they purchased this large building. It became home to a wide range of campaigns and groups, such as Women's Aid and the National Abortion Campaign (NAC), as well as WHRRIC, and provided a meeting place and conference centre for many feminist organisations. Ultimately, WHRRIC merged with the Women's Health Information Centre and the new organisation became known as Women's Health. Women's Health continued in existence until March 2006 when it closed due to lack of funding.

The nuts and bolts of the IWASG support system

Isabel Ros Lopez,[4] a Spanish feminist who came to London in 1978, joined Release in 1983, having first been a pregnancy counsellor at the Pregnancy Advisory Service. She became the worker designated to deal with abortion seekers from both Spain and Ireland when the organisation decided to collapse both services into one in 1983. Isabel speaks of where she picked up from Iris and her co-worker:

My brief included abortion work for Irish and Spanish women. Obviously, there was already a system in place. This is the gist of it: there was one telephone number which was listed in European editions of the Boston Women's Health Collective's handbook, Our Bodies, Ourselves, first published in 1969, which opened up new ground in empowering women to understand and take control of their health. A lot of the Spanish and some of the Irish abortion seekers came to know the IWASG and SWASG helpline numbers from this source. Also, the number was circulated on the Irish and Spanish feminist grapevine, in magazines, newsletters, on stickers surreptitiously pasted on the walls of public toilets, train stations, and the London Underground.

Many Irish women reported finding the necessary information in the ads pages of the British women's 'glossy', Cosmopolitan. Further, the clinics gave out helpline numbers to anyone needing them. To further augment the aura of stealth and concealment surrounding abortion support work, the code name, 'Imelda', was devised for the Irish Women's Abortion Support Group. This was used by women in Ireland after the ban on information was imposed by the Irish government in 1987, since it allowed them to talk about abortion without mentioning the word itself for fear of prosecution.

We had built up an information pack at Release for anyone covering the calls. If a woman was ringing us out of the blue without having consulted a doctor or counsellor in either Ireland or Spain, we would provide a full service for her, including arranging accommodation, whether in a B&B or with an IWASG or SWASG member. We had got training from the Pregnancy Advisory Service (PAS) on the precise information we needed to know, such as establishing whether a woman had had a pregnancy test, and if so, how long she was pregnant. We had checklists and forms to fill. We would then book an appointment for a consultation and counselling at the clinic. Remember, those were the days before mobile phones and it was often a dodgy business for a woman to be making furtive phone calls during daytime hours if she was at home, in school or college, or at work.

Kate Duke[5], a Northern Irish woman who joined IWASG in the 1980s, makes the point that as far as Southern Irish women were concerned, a clear distinction has to be made between pre and post-1987. Before 1987, many Irish women were given counselling, were seen by a doctor, and referred to clinics in Britain by either the Well Woman, the Irish Pregnancy Counselling Centre, or its successor, Open Door (subsequently known as Open Line) Counselling, and the Irish Family Planning Association, all based in Dublin. Northern Irish women, or even Southern women living in areas close to the Border, such as Donegal, Monaghan and Leitrim, could, if they had access to the necessary information, contact the Ulster Pregnancy Advisory Association or the Northern Irish Family Planning Association for pregnancy testing, counselling and referral to abortion clinics in Britain. These Northern Irish services remained legal, if inadequate to meet the demand, especially from women whose pregnancies were advanced. Kate Duke recalls:

Reading my notes from the time, I see that Open Line Counselling was forced to close in January 1987. The Well Woman Centre and the Irish Family Planning Association, although not obliged to put up the shutters and shut shop, seeing that both organisations offered a range of different health services to women, were subject to the same legal restrictions concerning abortion. The IWASG helpline set up in London became crucially important at this point. To begin with, it was the only link Southern Irish women had unless they had the necessary information to contact the clinics directly themselves. In November, 1987 the illegal underground Women's Information Network (WIN) was established in Dublin and this helped relieve the pressure on London. But that was only up to a point considering the massive increase in numbers coming to Britain during the 80s. Paradoxically, this was because of the amount of publicity being given in the media to the subject of abortion.

The IWASG helpline, based at WHRRIC in London, and operated by the worker there, was absolutely fantastic. Most of the calls were fielded by her, whether it was Blanca Fernandez, or later, Pat Thompson and a few others. In addition, a rota of IWASG members ran an evening service every Tuesday between 6 and 9 p.m. All of the volunteers on the evening service were Irish. The argument at the time (it changed later) went that the Irish women coming over might feel comforted by Irish voices.

I have lots of memories of those times. Something I do remember vividly while answering the phone is women whispering. You'd have to ask them to speak up, but of course they wouldn't; they were afraid of being overheard.

Writing in 1988 about their work, IWASG members state that extraordinary circumstances prevailed even before 1987 when a total ban on abortion information and referral services, as well as state censorship of publications and the media generally, were introduced in the Republic. They say that before the first of the five referenda on abortion in 1983, they dealt only with emergencies. This means that they helped women who found it difficult to cope with being in a big city like London, who needed financial support or accommodation, or who welcomed being visited while they were in the clinic. However, following the first referendum and a developing climate of fear in the Republic, it became increasingly the norm to fill the massive hole left by the removal of Open Line and the curtailing of the services of the Well Woman and the Family Planning Association.[6]

Kate Duke suggests that while making clinic appointments was one thing, dealing with even the most routine medical questions and offering advice, however cursory, required training. Volunteers sought this from the Pregnancy Advisory Service (PAS) and WHRRIC. Unlike Isabel Ros Lopez, for instance, who could depend on the expertise she accumulated during her years as a counsellor with PAS, most IWASG volunteers had little or no experience of the medical, social work or counselling fields in relation to terminations. Not until the enactment of the Regulation of Information Act of 1995 by the government of the Republic, which allowed for abortion information to be provided, was the situation eased.

In the course of her work Isabel recalls being very concerned about the fact that in some cases abortion seekers were being ripped off by cab drivers and unscrupulous maverick clinics. Women, she says, were taking incredible risks, like turning up out of the blue in London and asking cab drivers to take them to a clinic. Occasionally, excessive fares were being demanded and women were taken to all sorts of places. In some cases, these might be Harley Street clinics asking for very extravagant fees; in other cases women were taken to unsafe places, including backstreet abortionists.

It is also true that not all involved in facilitating abortions for Spanish and Irish women were as ethical as might be expected. In one instance, allegations of commissions being paid by a particular clinic for being favoured over others resulted in these stories filtering back to Spain. In consequence, an investigating committee from a feminist group in the Basque Country came to check out a rumour that a Spanish woman was bringing abortion seekers to a London clinic and pocketing commission.

When IWASG and SWASG were formed, Isabel Ros says, although they functioned as two separate groups, they had joint dealings with the clinics in order to get the best deals for women coming over from both countries. Regular checks and surveys were carried out to keep track of the clinical side. Also, surveys were conducted to discover women's experiences of the termination once they left the clinic. As a result, she concludes:

> Our monitoring of the clinics was an important service to its users and to services in Ireland and Spain helping women to get to London. Information flowed back and forth. We managed to get the crème de la crème of clinics. Our favourite was PAS, the Pregnancy Advisory Service, which was a feminist, non-profit making collective. I knew them very well as I had worked with them for some time as a pregnancy counsellor.

> We had a lot of dealings with PAS. We had an agreement on their charges based on the fact that Irish and Spanish women were already paying a lot in getting to London. Not only did they reduce their charges, but they also offered some free terminations which helped in cases of abortion seekers with severe money problems. We also used what were then private clinics, such as the Parkview in Ealing and The Leigham in Streatham, as well as those run by the charities, Marie Stopes, the Pregnancy Advisory Service (PAS) and the British Pregnancy Advisory Service (BPAS), the latter two merging in 1996 under the title of BPAS.

SPONSORED SWIM

for: OPENLINE COUNSELLING
organised _by:_ IRISH WOMENS ABORTION SUPPORT GROUP

on Saturday <u>NOVEMBER 1</u> from <u>3.30 - 5.30</u>

at MONTEM POOL,
    HORNSEY RD., N7.

(Nearest tube: Finsbury Park)

<u>OPENLINE COUNSELLING</u>, Dublin, provide information and counselling for women who want abortions, referring them to London for the operation.

THE IRISH WOMEN' ABORTION SUPPORT GROUP, a group of Irish women here, provides accomadation and support for those women during their stay.

<u>Openline Counselling</u> is in dire financial straits. Last year both they and the Well Women Centre faced charges of anti constitutional behaviour in referring women here for abortions. This case is due to be heard this October and has meant massive added expense. A very valuable and much used service is under threat.

I.W.A.S.C., Co Women's Reproductive Rights Information Centre,
52-54 Featherstone St., Lon. E.C.1

Swimming for Open Line

Isabel Ros Lopez 'Keeping Irish Women Well and the Line Open'!

Isabel recollects that a Spanish woman died in 1984 in what was ultimately discovered to be the Parkview Clinic in Ealing (then a private clinic before being taken over by the charity, Marie Stopes International). Although the death was accidental, she says:

> We pursued the matter until we found out what clinic it was, and exactly what had happened. We had a meeting with Kenneth Clarke when he was Minister of Health in the Tory government of the time. It was important to do this kind of work, not only from a humanitarian point of view, but to raise awareness. Keeping tabs on the clinics meant that we kept them on their toes. We came up with a lot of detailed information, statistics and such which we circulated amongst relevant organisations in Ireland and Spain.

> We worked out how much Irish and Spanish women were spending, taking all their expenses into account. We also calculated how much the Spanish and Irish states were gaining in terms of savings on health services, not to speak of how much, what were then nationally owned airlines, Aer Lingus and Iberia, were making from fares. Then there were airport taxes, etc. And this didn't even take into account the cost to Irish and Spanish women's mental and physical health, given the secrecy, the hassle and pressure women were subjected to.

Cross border co-operation – Open Line and the Well Woman in Dublin

Isabel Ros Lopez considers that the formation of SWASG and IWASG in London, their connection with Irish, Spanish and British pro-choice organisations supporting reproductive rights, and their regular contact with British abortion providers were crucial for Irish and Spanish abortion seekers, especially in the 'bad old days' of censorship and repression. She recollects the contacts she had with Ruth Riddick of Open Line before it was closed down in 1987, and with

Noreen Byrne of the Well Woman Centre in Dublin. Isabel recalls: 'We were in constant contact with them, we were always feeding off each other's energy, trying to find solutions. This was part of feminist internationalism or cross-border co-operation in action.'

Noreen Byrne,[7] who was Director of the Well Woman in Dublin, and subsequently became chairperson of the National Women's Council, remembers:

> *I joined the Well Woman in 1980, and in 1982 I became the Director after the founder, Anne Connolly, left the organisation. Whatever contacts Anne Connolly had with a support system in England, it was probably on an individual basis, but I wanted to establish a link that was more organised and political. It was at that point that I came to be in touch with IWASG. It's hard to think back, but I remember that it coincided with a lot of feminist political activity going on around Northern Ireland at the time. Women Against Imperialism had been formed in West Belfast in 1978, an organisation which highlighted gender politics, and particularly the Armagh women prisoners' 'dirty protest'. This had put the role of the female body in political struggle in the spotlight.*

> *When I look back I recall that there was a group of women who were in a minority amongst the Irish in Britain, but were militant and willing to work politically around the abortion question. What was so interesting for me was that they were women who were completely comfortable in the practice of their politics in the sense of doing the practical work. They received women from Ireland, put them up, looked after them as human beings, even told lies for them if things needed to be covered up, bought gifts for them to take back to Ireland so they could camouflage the purpose of their visit to London – to give them an alibi, to fool their families – so to speak.*

> *After making a lonely and difficult decision to have an abortion, women went over to London and encountered a whole bunch of women who didn't give a damn who*

thought what about them, they were just going to do this practical work. It was just amazing. Many of the IWASG members were young, some were lesbians who probably had to get out of Ireland themselves and knew what it was like to be 'on the run'. They didn't necessarily share each other's politics generally speaking, but once the phone call came from a woman needing help, whoever was on the rota rolled into action. For me, having been involved in left-wing politics as a woman, it was the first time I came across sisterhood – feminism in practice.

Isabel bears out this concern for abortion seekers:

As well as liaising with the clinic on behalf of the women callers, everything possible was done to make their stay in London tolerable. This is where the Abortion Support Groups came in. They held meetings perhaps once a month, sometimes more frequently. Rotas were devised at the meetings with, say, two, sometimes three people each month making themselves available to collect women from airports and railway stations when necessary, escort them to the clinic, put them up, make them feel at ease, etc.

Language-wise and culture-wise, both groups had the same aim: to make women feel comfortable and safe. Everyone in the Spanish group spoke the language. On occasion we had women from Ireland staying with people from the Spanish group because they didn't want to be with someone from Ireland. Sometimes abortion seekers felt they were taking a big risk staying with someone from home. Ireland, in particular, is a very small country with a small population, and close by. The chances of running into someone who knows you is not that remote. However, Spanish women also had to worry about encountering someone they knew at a Spanish airport. There were even instances of people meeting up on the plane. You have to remember that explaining away a trip to London was a little more difficult for Spanish women. Irish women could always say they were visiting their brother/sister/aunt/uncle, etc., or were just on a shopping trip!

Blanca Fernandez[8] was an employee of WHRICC beginning in 1987. She took on the abortion support work until she left the organisation in 1996. Blanca, who had a background working as a counsellor with the Pregnancy Advisory Service (PAS), recalls that support work often required considerable inputs of time and energy. She says that in cases where an Irish or Spanish abortion seeker felt unable to negotiate the London public transport system, either she herself or a member of one of the support groups would pick the woman up from Heathrow and deliver her to the member providing the support service on that occasion. Blanca recalls that the switch-over frequently took place at Holborn Tube Station and that such arrangements often involved considerable co-ordination and fine tuning. However, she says:

The level of commitment at the time was phenomenal. Both IWASG and SWASG women were grassroots activists in the real sense of the word. They would turn their hand to anything, whether the nitty-gritty of meeting women, taking them to the clinic, producing leaflets, stickers, banners and posters, or addressing meetings and conferences highlighting the plight of abortion seekers and raising money for them. This was real sisterhood and they didn't get – or expect – any glory or medals for it. We should never forget the part they played in extending a helping hand to the women of Ireland and Spain.

Pat Thompson,[9] a British woman of African Caribbean descent, who joined Women's Health in 1990, and was the Health Information Manager for fourteen years, frequently dealt with calls from Ireland. Pat recounts that before she joined Women's Health she was also a pregnancy counsellor for PAS for five years from 1985 to 1990 where one of her tasks was what was known as THUS counselling. THUS referred to The Heathrow Unit Service bus, which for some years PAS organised on Fridays to collect groups of abortion seekers from Ireland and elsewhere, to transport them to the PAS consulting rooms located at Charlotte Street in London's

West End. Here, the women saw a counsellor and finally two doctors.

As significant numbers of these Irish women had never travelled outside Ireland before in the 1980s and early 1990s and were unfamiliar with the London transport system, an IWASG member often accompanied them on board the bus from Heathrow. Pat says she also helped assist in arrangements for overnight stay, whether at B&B accommodation close to the PAS clinic in Richmond, or with IWASG members. Help was at hand to direct or escort women to the clinic on Saturdays, and equally on Sunday mornings, when women were discharged and made their way back to Ireland.

Inevitably, not all ran smoothly. Ann Hayes,[10] an IWASG member, relates the problems sometimes attached to meeting women at the airport. 'There were often really farcical as well as poignant situations', she remembers. 'I had this long red skirt that I used to wear so that women could easily identify me amongst the waiting crowds, many of them taxi drivers with clipboards and printed flyers looking for "Mr. X" or "Mr. Y". I didn't want to be cutting up a cornflake box and holding it up with someone's name on it at the passenger exit at Heathrow, announcing to all the world that such-and-such a one was here. While nobody at Heathrow would be remotely interested, the woman herself might feel intimidated.'

Ann recalls that when social workers in Ireland, and occasionally the Well Woman or Open Line, sent women to IWASG, they would sometimes underestimate their knowledge of London. 'You have to meet her [whatever her name]; she won't be able to manage', they would say. 'Then you might find on meeting the woman that she had been to London loads of times. That used to drive me spare. Half a day spent travelling all the way out to Heathrow and back when I could have met her at Holborn, or wherever', she says.

Gautam Appa,[11] Ann Rossiter's partner, recalls the times he spent ferrying abortion seekers to the clinics:

Occasionally I drove women staying with us to the clinics in the early hours of the morning when they specifically requested it. Sometimes it was because their money had run out, or it was a difficult journey to make because they were unused to negotiating London trains, tubes and buses, or they just felt too unwell to take public transport. Ann, my partner, didn't drive. After having spent the night with us, women were more at their ease and things went smoothly. However, I have to say that in the 1980s, and even in the 1990s when Ireland was getting to be less mono-cultural, numbers of women from Ireland were visibly shocked on arriving into a mixed race household. I don't think they had even been that up close to a black person before.

It was clear that sometimes women found it difficult to communicate with me, even though the conversation was invariably very general, very mundane really, like asking them about their preferences in beverages or food. Once or twice I came in for some stick. In particular, I remember being rebuked by a woman who had been made pregnant by a Pakistani man on 'a one-night stand'. For some reason I was expected to take the blame because I'm from the Indian sub-continent! It was a bit hard staying mute, especially when I found myself driving this woman right from Forest Gate in the far reaches of London's East End, where we used to live, to Richmond, just beyond the borders of West London, at about 6 a.m. In total this was about a three-hour round trip at that time of day, especially as I hit the rush hour on the way home. All for the cause, I suppose.

Pat Thompson says that she was particularly struck by the similarities between African-Caribbean and Irish women in relation to abortion. Black women, she says, have been raised to believe that abortion is a dirty word. 'You were trained and socialised to go ahead with the pregnancy', although, she points out that in her case the views of her pro-choice mother had a considerable impact, such that she entered the field of abortion counselling. She identifies the influence of the black churches in stigmatising abortion. She also suggests that the history of slavery and the intense struggle involved in staying alive, let alone sustaining the family unit, is bound to have left its mark. Pat argues that she empathised with the deeply emotional stories related to her in the course of her counselling of Irish and black women. Interestingly, she relates:

> I believe that I have lived quite closely with Irish women and the intense struggle they have with themselves in deciding whether or not to have an abortion. I feel I understand the cultural inferences, the weight of their history. After all, it is in some ways a mirror image of my own.

Fund-raising activities

Fund-raising activities were a permanent feature of IWASG. In fact, fund-raising, campaigning and liaison with the various pro-choice organisations in Ireland were all of a piece. Ann Hayes describes the situation with regard to financially straitened abortion seekers who requested help with travel expenses or clinic fees:

> We have had many middle class women, a considerable number of whom were students, come to IWASG with money difficulties. We have also had poor, working-class women whose circumstances are such that they have had to borrow heavily for their abortion and travel expenses.

> It is not unknown for women to borrow from loan sharks who lend at extortionate rates of interest and operate on housing estates all over Ireland. These are women who are unable to get credit through banks, building societies, etc. We have had cases of women getting money from credit unions ostensibly for kitting out their kids for their First Communion or Confirmation ceremonies, but using it for their abortion. Even women who are relatively well-heeled and well-travelled often find that getting hold of such a large sum of money in a hurry is a difficult proposition. It is not unusual to find that they have to tell elaborate cover stories to get loans from friends and relatives.

Equally demanding was the extensive fundraising in support of defensive actions on the part of pro-choice groups and students' unions in the Republic of Ireland. These were ranged against the Society for the Protection of the Unborn Child (SPUC) in its ultimately successful attempt to stop pregnancy counselling and abortion referral in the period 1987-1995.

In the process of raising money, every effort was made to publicise the situation in Ireland, north and south of the border, and to seek support for organisations in the front line there. Newspaper and journal articles were an important vehicle for disseminating information and for raising donations. Consequently, considerable time and effort was invested in acquiring the knowledge needed to brief journalists, or indeed, for IWASG members to write news items, leaflets and reports themselves. British feminist magazines and journals, such as *Spare Rib*, *Outwrite* and *Feminist Review* reported on Irish abortion issues at various times, but also more mainstream women's magazines such as *Cosmopolitan* gave coverage.

An example of a briefing was an 'Information Day' held on 7th December 1985. This involved updating by specialists, such as counsellors, clinic personnel or members of the various Irish agencies on the legal aspects of abortion in Ireland, North and South. They also provided relevant medical information, including procedures followed at abortion clinics, and the giving of emotional support to abortion seekers pre and post-termination.[12]

Another example of information provision is recorded in a report of a meeting held on 22nd September 1985, where Noreen Byrne, Director of the Well Woman Centre in Dublin, addressed an audience including the London Irish Women's Centre, the London Armagh Group (the British-based support group for republican women prisoners), the Spanish Women's Abortion Support Group, and IWASG. The discussion concerned the legal and political developments stemming from a national referendum enabling the government of the Republic of Ireland to insert a foetal civil rights amendment into its constitution in 1983, thus placing the rights of the foetus and those of the woman bearing it on an equal basis. Noreen explained in detail the response of pro-choice organisations, including her own, the Well Woman Centre, and of the Woman's Right to Choose Group formed in Dublin in 1979, as well as the broader movement, the Anti-Amendment Campaign, which followed. A further briefing by Noreen took place in January 1986, and this was followed by a press conference held at Conway Hall in Holborn, central London, hosted by IWASG.[13]

The extent of the monies needing to be raised is put into perspective when account is taken of the fact that £80,000 in legal costs had to be met by the Well Woman and Open Line to fight the case brought by the Society for the Protection of the Unborn Child. While IWASG was merely one of the organisations worldwide contributing to relieve this massive financial burden, minutes of meetings at the time note numerous events taking place before and after the legal ruling. These were in the form of benefits, sponsored swims and walks. Benefits were held in a variety of places; posters and leaflets which survive mention a 'Defend the Clinics' *lá féile Bríd* (St. Brigid's Day) event on 1st February 1985 in honour of Brigid's work on fertility and a women-only disco featuring 'The Guest Stars' at Islington Town Hall.[14] On the day preceding, the 31st January, Noreen Byrne held a press conference hosted by IWASG at Conway Hall, Red Lion Square, London.

In July 1986 SWASG, the Spanish women's group, organised one of many *céilí* benefits at the London Irish Centre in Camden Town. An ingeniously worded leaflet demanding, 'Keep Women Well in Ireland and the Line Open' scripted by Isabel Ros Lopez in reference to the closing down of Open Line and terminating the abortion referral service at the Well Woman in Dublin (see poster on page 102). Featuring *Sistahs in Song, Ginger and Spice*, as well as a puppet show, the leaflet urged women to attend the benefit at Caxton House in Archway.[15] A sponsored swim was held specifically to aid Open Line at Clissold Park Baths in July

1986 followed by another at Montem Pool, Hornsey Road on 1st November[16] (see poster on page 101). Minutes of 12th June 1986 mention that £800 had been sent to the campaign in Dublin and the next month's meeting minutes note that a further £336 was being sent. A plaintive note by the minute taker at the former meeting states: 'Lately, our main function [apart from the support of abortion seekers] seems to be fund raising – is this enough?'[17]

The role of the Workers' Beer Company in IWASG fund-raising

Many of those interviewed for this book recalled the fund-raising events, both for abortion seekers and to support the campaigns in Ireland. Catherine Boyle,[18] one IWASG member, was a 'dab hand' at quenching punters' thirst at music gigs, particularly those served by the Workers' Beer Company. The Company was set up in 1985 by Battersea and Wandsworth Trades Council in South London as a fundraising arm of the labour and trade union movement. Its aim was to give support to the campaigning and solidarity work of grassroots organisations and, in this respect, its patronage was invaluable to IWASG in its endeavours. Catherine recollects:

> A regular means of fund-raising that we used was serving in the beer tents for the Workers' Beer Company. These beer tents were erected at gigs like the fleádh (Irish music festival) in Finsbury Park, North London, the May Day Festival on Clapham Common, South London which was attended by many trade unionists and radicals, and the Reading and Leeds festivals. Also, there was the Glastonbury pop festival spread over four days. I used to have to get a team of twelve together and wages were donated to IWASG.

> Many in the team were not IWASG members, but mainly Irish young men and women that I met around the Kilburn High Road, in pubs, or at different events like the

Kilburn Youth Festival which I helped to organise each summer. Sometimes my son and his mates came along. They were doing it for a good cause and the draw for them (and for me) was free entry to the festivals to hear bands like REM and the Manic Street Preachers they couldn't afford to see otherwise. There's nothing quite like experiencing a band in the flesh. Tickets, if you could get them, were £70, £80, or even a hundred quid for Glastonbury at the time.

I did all the organising, running through the work routines, trying to make sure people turned up and on time, and that they were well rehearsed. It was hard work pulling pints under a plastic roof as the tent got hot and clammy with the crowds. You can imagine what it was like if we got hot weather. If it had rained before the festival started it was muddy underfoot and you had to drag your feet behind the bar 'til they nearly dropped off. I just used to think of the cause. More often than not I thought about some very vulnerable woman I had helped out, and that gave me the impetus to carry on. Also, the money was good. At a time when bar workers were getting £3.50 an hour we were getting £4.50 and sometimes more.

Connections with Irish community organisations

Other than the Irish, British and Spanish organisations mentioned above, IWASG had contact with a number of others, notably the London Irish Women's Centre, and to a lesser extent, Action Group for Irish Youth (AIGY).

The London Irish Women's Centre (LIWC)

When, after three years in temporary accommodation, the London Irish Women's Centre (LIWC) opened in 1986 at its dedicated premises on Stoke Newington Church Street in North East London, many activists felt that Irish feminism in London had arrived. There was great excitement at the opening which was attended by the journalist, Nell McCafferty, Ireland's most famous feminist. Although Breda Gray, in her article on Irish identity in 1980s London, is probably somewhat off the mark in saying that it was established as 'a central co-ordinating body for Irish women's groups',[1] since feminist groups in Britain organised autonomously, the Centre was nonetheless a focal point. Marian Larragy,[20] an IWASG member, has fond memories of both the place and the people in its early days:

> *Founder members, the Dowd sisters, Rae and Eilish, were from Northern Ireland. As well as all the nitty gritty of the welfare, educational and cultural services the Centre provided, Rae later developed a specialism in alternative therapies, like massage, and was invited by lots of groups to give demonstrations on how a massage is done. Coming from a large family, she always had this great awareness of how hard it can be for women to accept this kind of caring and tenderness, when so many have been taught to give but not to receive.*

> *Brid Boland was the great traditional Irish musician, as well as researcher, writer and educationalist. Between them, Brid, the Dowds and others, the women of the Centre encompassed a range of traditional and new feminist values.*

> *Angela (Angie Birtill), came later to the Centre and, I think, came from a different political tradition. She was well versed in all the important political issues of the day, and she made some really crucial connections with second-generation Irish women, being British-born herself, as well as with the trade unions. You saw the LIWC banner everywhere, whether at pickets of the Irish Embassy over the lack of reproductive rights in Ireland, and at the Armagh Group and Stop the Strip Searches protests regarding the treatment of republican prisoners. The LIWC banner was also visible outside the Royal Courts of Justice in support of Southall Black Sisters and Justice for*

Enjoying the second London Irish Women's
Centre Conference, 1985
© Joanne O'Brien

*Women's protest in 1992 at Kiranjit Ahluwalia's life
sentence over murdering her abusive husband. I also know
that the Centre was involved with the setting up of Sólás
Anois, the Irish women's refuge from domestic violence.*

Regarding the issue of abortion and LIWC, anecdotal
evidence acquired by IWASG members from abortion seekers
over the years suggests that traditional or mainstream Irish
community organisations, such as the Camden and the
Hammersmith Irish Centres, have at times received requests
for information, and sometimes help, and that the type of
reply received – whether helpful or dismissive – depended on
who answered the call. Certainly, none of these centres have
had a formal policy of extending a helping hand to Irish
women in their search for a termination. As discussed in
Chapter 3, this is despite having received funding from
bodies, such as the GLC, which had a progressive policy on
reproductive rights. LIWC was, however, exceptional in this
respect. Angie Birtill,[21] who worked at the Centre as a

115

Housing, Employment and Welfare Rights adviser for twelve years, from 1988 to 2000, had this to say:

As far as I know, IWASG never requested a base at the LIWC but some of the centre's workers were members of IWASG or took part in the rota of providing accommodation for women coming over from Ireland. So there was a lot of cross-fertilisation of ideas and activities at this time. I also believe attempts were made to obtain funding for abortion support work. A meeting was held with someone from the GLC but funding was refused on the grounds that women coming from Ireland were not British residents, and were therefore ineligible for funding. In some ways this refusal was instrumental in getting the LIWC off the ground as the original founders left that meeting with thoughts about applying for funds to meet the need of Irish women who were living in this country.

Brid Boland,[22] one of the Centre's early workers, recalls that the embryonic Irish Women's Centre first shared an office with the Cinema of Women in 1983, a British feminist organisation, and later acquired an office in an industrial building until, with the help of the late Bernie Grant, the African Caribbean MP for Tottenham, the dedicated building on Stoke Newington Church Street opened in 1986. She recounts that from its early beginnings staff had a list of the IWASG support rota on hand for anyone calling the Centre regarding an abortion. She also recalls that IWASG ran a workshop at virtually all of the Centre's annual conferences, in 1984, 1985, 1987, 1988, 1989. Unfortunately, however, it has to be said that, despite its mental health implications for Irish women, especially in maintaining life-long secrecy, a point discussed throughout this book, abortion was not an issue addressed at the Centre's most recent conference held in 1998 on Irish women, the topic being mental health. Neither was it included as an issue in the Centre's profile of Irish Women in London, *Roots & Realities*, published in 1993.[23]

Angie Birtill continues her account:

Once the Centre got going the main demands on our time were from women who were homeless or living in really bad housing conditions. We provided practical help for women experiencing domestic violence and to women who were refused welfare benefits to which they were legally entitled. We dealt with race and sex discrimination in the workplace and worked with Travellers living in Hackney and other parts of London. We were always inundated with demands for this kind of work but we also took regular calls from women in Ireland who wanted information about getting an abortion in London. The IWASG rota was invaluable for assisting these women.

Reproductive rights for women was one of the essential principles underlying the LIWC's work. We stated this principle in our publications and in speeches at the meetings of other organisations to which we were invited. Furthermore, we joined other women's groups in publicly demonstrating outside the Irish Embassy at the time of the X case in Ireland.

Brid Boland stresses that it was possible for LIWC to demonstrate at such events because the Centre did not have charitable status (this was adopted after 2000). She says:

Restrictions would have been placed on the LIWC once it became registered with charitable status. Extensive investigation was carried out by LIWC on this over many years, i.e. meetings with legal advisors, etc. by individual staff (i.e. fundraiser), and at least once, a meeting between a legal advisor, LIWC staff, and management. Until at least the late 1990s, it was considered by the Centre that many activities and positions, for example, attendance at political-type demonstrations, and participation in any campaigns that challenged government policy in some areas, would be detrimental.

Action Group for Irish Youth (AGIY)

Amongst other organisations which proved exceptional were those with a feminist ethos, such as Irish Women in Islington, the Wandsworth Irish Women's Group, and Irish Women's Perspectives. Another organisation which proved exceptional was the Action Group for Irish Youth (AGIY), based in the Holloway Road in North London, which received occasional telephone calls from abortion seekers in Ireland as a result of the Group's publication, *Survival: A Guide to London for Young Irish People*. Exceptionally for Irish community publications, the guide listed IWASG and its services, as well as listing Women's Health and BPAS, an abortion provider.

Brian McCarthy,[24] who worked at AGIY for most of the 1990s, and who was involved in researching and producing its guide, points out:

The management committee of AGIY was composed of people you could call 'new wave'. They were progressive on social issues, not least gay rights and reproductive rights, and information on groups active on these and myriad other issues, including HIV/Aids, were listed in the guide. However, when abortion information was outlawed in the Republic, we had to produce two different versions of the Guide so that it wouldn't be confiscated like when copies of The Guardian newspaper and Cosmopolitan magazine were removed from newsagents. Remember, we distributed the guide in Ireland as well as in Britain to try and inform and prepare young Irish people for emigration.

Our funding came from a variety of sources, including the London Borough Grants, FAS (Training and Employment Authority, Ireland), Dion (Irish Government) and the Ireland Fund of Great Britain, but from the Irish side, especially from Dion, there was never any complaint about listing abortion services, at least not to my knowledge. Of course, the guide was about giving information, not offering a support service like IWASG. Also, AGIY was not a campaigning group.

In sum, the support work of IWASG encapsulated the contributions – almost always way beyond the call of duty – of a wide spectrum of organisations, British, Irish, and Spanish in particular, and their personnel based in Britain and in Ireland. These ranged across health and reproductive rights organisations, abortion providers, women's centres, and women's voluntary groups. Only slowly is recognition of this multi-layered web of support coming to be spoken of beyond those 'in the know', i.e. beyond the narrow confines of pro-choice circles.

The extent of this multi-layered web is emphasised by Marella Buckley, writing in 1997 in a collection of essays on emigration and Irish identities. Buckley emphasises the extent of the web, from the services offered by IWASG, to the supportive atmosphere towards Irish abortion seekers to be found in English guest-houses in the vicinity of clinics run by sympathetic families 'who are used to receiving Irish girls and women who are *on the run* in this way.'[25] The web is stretched even further by Evelyn Mahon, Catherine Conlon and Lucy Dillon, the authors of the 1998 report on crisis pregnancies for the Irish Department of Health and Children, who speak warmly of the guest houses or B&B establishments: '...the owners...usually offer to collect women from and return them to the airport...Knowing that the staff at the B&B are in some way connected to the clinic makes women feel more comfortable as they do not feel the need to conceal their reasons for being in England.'[26]

CHAPTER 6

The Irish abortion seeker as a 'special case'

The comments made by the writer Marella Buckley in the previous chapter also extend to the distress of Irish women displayed on arrival at British abortion clinics. Buckley argues that clinic staff have 'an intense and supportive awareness of the traumatised condition of Irish women', who, she says, are considered poles apart from British and overseas abortion seekers. She makes the case that the counselling women receive takes into account 'the extra layers of trauma' that Irish women experience, particularly the need for secrecy before and after their termination. She concludes that in Ireland there is no acknowledgement of the assistance given by the health care system to Irish women 'in their desperate migrations across the water'[1]

Those 'extra layers of trauma' have been the subject of some debate and even disagreement over interpretation within IWASG itself. Mary Sexton,[2] a long-time member of the group from Northern Ireland, and with lengthy experience as a nurse and counsellor working in abortion clinics in both the private and National Health sectors, insists that at base the Irish abortion seekers she encountered were no different from any others. Amongst the various nationalities and ethnic groups she counselled and nursed, few, if any, she says, wished to trumpet their abortion experience to the world at large, given the stigma attached in most, if not all, societies. In other words, secrecy was not exclusive to Irish women.

Mary's patients, Irish and otherwise, worried about the decision they had made, an ambivalence which, she says, was detectable right across the board. Their worries were heavily focused on surviving the operation itself, given that many had never been under anaesthetic before. Despite nurses and doctors assuring them of the statistical improbability of their demise or becoming ill from a termination procedure, she says that abortion seekers, regardless of nationality or background, fretted over the impact on their families, and in particular on their children, if they had them, should matters end badly. She says:

> I had experience in nursing and counselling women from Britain, Ireland and elsewhere in Europe from the late 70s and through to 1983 when I stopped nursing and became a social worker. In my experience Irish women were much like any other: they were making a major decision in their life; they worried about what would happen to them or their children if anything went wrong with the abortion, or on their journey. Also, like women everywhere, they didn't want to broadcast their decision to have an abortion.

Pauline O'Hare, a Northern Irish member of IWASG who spent eight years as a pregnancy counsellor at PAS, also argues strongly for the normalization of Irish abortion seekers in addressing their counselling needs at a conference held in May 1997 at Ruskin College, Oxford. She says:

> Firstly, I would say that there is not a great deal of difference between Irish woman and English women in terms of counselling...There is a misconception that I want to discuss first however that exists within English clinics, that somehow Irish woman are very different. You often hear the word 'backward', meaning that Irish people are backward in terms of abortion. This gives the impression that the Irish are like the old Victorian depictions of 'lesser' people with their knuckles trailing the ground, and simian-like features! In contrast to this caricature of the Irish, I would like to give some reasons for the difference in the approach to abortion in Ireland and in Britain.[3]

Pauline places in context the reasons, she believes, underpin what for many is the conundrum of Irish attitudes to abortion, some of which already have been outlined in Chapter 2. Amongst the reasons she highlights are British colonialism, the Great Famine of the mid-nineteenth century which resulted in a million fatalities and was the catalyst for a continuous pattern of emigration, and a population consistently depleted of its youth, and thus deprived of the dynamics of change. She mentions the effect of the Irish Civil War and the partitioning of the country, the power of the churches, the lack of significant urbanisation, and the strong family ties. She points out, by way of contrast to Irish women, the massive changes wrought in British women's lives, not least in attitudes to sexuality and fertility, as a result of large-scale female industrial employment and their mobilisation in two world wars.

With regard to the counselling of Irish abortion seekers, Pauline argues that such women 'are very clear in their decision because they have obviously spent quite a lot of money in getting this far...so counselling over whether someone has made the right choice is not an issue.'[4] She then makes a point which may well have a bearing on how Irish women are perceived at the clinics: 'you still find that they do want to talk quite a bit about how they made their decision, when they found out they were pregnant, how they fell pregnant, what happened, how they got the money together, and just every aspect of it.'[5]

This outpouring to a counsellor from women who are likely agitated and nervous following their journey, and in the presence of a stranger, however, sympathetic, may well be regarded as unconventional, a departure from the norm. Pauline suggests that this may be the first opportunity for numbers of Irish women to talk about their abortion decision. 'In my experience', she says, 'those people who have not told anyone...about the issue are more likely to suffer trauma than somebody who has a good network of friends who they can tell...'[6]

In another attempt to place Irish women's abortion experience in context, the survey, *The Other Irish Journey*, co-authored by Ann Rossiter and Mary Sexton, and reproduced at the end of this volume, highlights the stressful nature of the journey to and from London – and *within* the city itself – and suggests that it is a prime factor in setting Irish women apart. In comparing their sample of Irish and non-Irish interviewees questioned at several clinics, the authors stress the similarities they found between the two groups: the difficulties encountered with GPs, the need to maintain secrecy beyond a small, intimate circle, problems in getting time off work, and so on.

In support of their argument, the authors of the survey quote Janet Hadley[7] in her book on abortion worldwide, where she states that although abortion is discussed as an *issue*, and is a stock element in soap opera crises from Coronation Street to EastEnders, it is still something of a taboo subject and hardly mentioned in everyday conversation in Britain when it relates to an individual's own experience. The point is also made in the survey that women in Britain (in particular, those living in London) are no longer a homogenous group (if they ever were). Distinctions need to be made, it is suggested, between the various groupings, whether African Caribbean, African, Indian, Pakistani, Chinese, Irish, English, etc., both British born and reared, as well those born elsewhere but now settled in Britain. All of these bring with them diverse social histories and contexts.

Contrasting the impact of religion on Irish, Spanish and other nationalities

When discussing the demeanour of Irish women with non-Irish activists and workers in the pro-choice field for the writing of this volume, it was noteworthy that while all highlighted the similarities, they also stressed the differences. Isobel Ros Lopez and Blanca Fernandez, for instance, on the basis of their years of abortion counselling work at PAS, pointed out that Spanish women also had to undertake the journey to London in difficult circumstances. They also had to resort to subterfuge, even to the extent of lying to people known to them that they met on the flight to London.

Without a significant ex-pat community in Britain, it was not so easy for Spanish women to brush off their sojourn in London as an 'away day' to attend a birthday party, a child's communion or confirmation day, or even as a 'brief shopping trip', as might be the case for many Irish women with relatives living in Britain.

Isabel Ros and Blanca highlighted the fact that Spanish women also had financial difficulties, and, over and above their Irish counterparts, most likely they understood or spoke little, if any, English. They also referred to the fact that significant numbers of them had the added pressure of being eighteen weeks pregnant and over, even after 1984 when the Spanish *Cortez* passed a law legalising abortion in limited circumstances. This was mostly due to delays in women getting together sufficient money for the trip before cheap flights became available, and for clinic fees which increased as the gestation period advanced.

In their interviews, both Isabel Ros and Blanca expressed the view that Irish women had internalised the strictures of the Catholic Church (not forgetting the strictures of the Protestant evangelical churches) to a much greater degree than their Spanish counterparts. They also suggested that Irish women were more heavily influenced by family attitudes than Spanish women. A reason for this degree of difference, they argued, was that Spanish women, feminist or not, had been caught up willy-nilly in a remarkable push for social change in the post-fascist era following Franco's death in 1975. The gradual dismantling of the fascist and patriarchal system in place after the Spanish Civil War, and the opening up of society to progressive, and even radical ideas, all played their part.

The changed landscape for Spanish women, albeit not as far reaching as many would have wished, meant that basic reforms which took other democratic countries from the end of the Second World War to the 1970s, were achieved in less than ten years in Spain. A combination of the women's movement, the Socialist Party (PSOE), the Communist Party

(PCE), and even centrist parties like the Democratic Centre Union (UCD) made this possible.

It also has to be remembered that an underground anti-fascist movement, including a women's movement, had operated long before the demise of Franco which meant that progressive ideas were being debated in the society at large, although furtively. In describing the history and politics of the period, the academics and feminist movement activists, Maria Angeles Duran and Maria Teresa Gallego,[8] stress that the Spanish Catholic Church, although still resolutely opposed to abortion, took a stand in favour of the transition to democracy post-Franco and was responsive to new egalitarian ideas about women, such as the stipulation in the new constitution of 1978 that outlaws gender discrimination.

While not wishing to dismiss either side of the argument, it has to be said that the historical and political differences between Ireland and Spain are considerable. Although the truth of the matter might have been a bit more complex, historically the Irish Catholic Church at grassroots level was never perceived as being in cahoots with the colonial power. This contrasted dramatically with Spain, where in the twentieth century the Spanish Catholic Church provided a major plank for the powers that be, i.e. for the fascist dictatorship.

As far as fascism in Ireland is concerned, first and foremost, as the historian and journalist, Tim Pat Coogan,[9] has emphasised, the authoritarian basis underpinning fascism was undoubtedly apparent in elements of Irish Catholicism. The former *Garda* (police) Commissioner O'Duffy, the leader of the Blueshirts, Ireland's own fascist movement, did indeed parade his brigades around the country displaying fascist insignia and executing Hitler salutes. He even led a 700-strong Irish Brigade to Spain in aid of the regime, and, with the blessing of the Catholic Church, determined to defeat the communists, 'the anti-Christ'. However, neither the agrarian forces, nor a significant body of big businessmen necessary to support such a movement, emerged in the southern Irish state during the period from the late 1920s to the mid-1930s to enable it to take root. Consequently, there was no intensive questioning of the Irish Catholic Church as occurred in Spain in the 1970s post-Franco. In fact, the Spanish Church felt impelled to re-invent itself and to accommodate the democratic forces fashioning the new Spain, if it were to survive as a significant entity at all.

A second reason why Ireland is different is that historically Catholicism was popularly identified as a badge of resistance, the proscribed and persecuted faith of an oppressed people. This contrasts with the position in Spain and also in Italy where opposition to the Catholic Church has been widespread for a century or more. For instance, the *risorgimento*, or nineteenth-century nationalist and anti-feudal movement aimed at unifying the eight separate states of the Italian peninsula, was fundamentally anti-clerical.[10] Furthermore, the *risorgimento* stood for the destruction of the Pope's temporal power – his feudal dominion over the Papal States which stretched from sea to sea across the peninsula.

The differences are perhaps best illustrated in two of the major personalities of Italian and Irish popular movements. On the one hand, Garibaldi (1807-1882), the legendary leader of the *risorgimento*, dressed dramatically in his customary red shirt and poncho, passionately denouncing the priests as no better than wolves and assassins, and the Pope as a bogus Christian. By contrast, Daniel O'Connell (1775-1847), the celebrated Irish leader known as the 'Liberator' and 'Ireland's uncrowned monarch', cut an altogether different figure. O'Connell, barrister, politician, and orator who championed the cause of Catholic emancipation in 'monster' meetings throughout Ireland, was far from being anticlerical. O'Connell enlisted the active support of the clergy in granting civil rights to Catholics through his Catholic Association. He also enlisted their help in gathering the monthly 'penny rent' or 'Catholic rent' levelled voluntarily on the peasant farmers. This was to finance a range of endeavours, including the purchase of school books, the education of Catholic priests and the legal protection of Catholics, and their political representation.[11]

Catholic emancipation was achieved by 1829 and the Church's role in rebuilding a shattered Ireland after the Great Famine set in motion a 'devotional revolution' which had the effect of further cementing the relationship between priests and people.[12] The partitioning of Ireland by Britain in 1921 served to reinforce the Church's influence. Since the majority in the new southern state were Catholics, few concessions were deemed necessary in the way of pluralism in the institutions of state, in the education system, or in the culture generally. A similar situation occurred in Northern Ireland with the creation of 'a Protestant state for a Protestant people', despite the territory's large Catholic minority.

If anything, Partition strengthened the position of the evangelical Protestant churches at the expense of the more moderate Church of Ireland (the Anglican Church), Britain's state religion. It has been argued that for all Northern Irish Protestants, even those *not* belonging to evangelical churches, such as Ian Paisley's Free Presbyterians, 'the explanatory power of fundamentalist religion resonates with the experience of [perceived] persecution, and of violence [from republicans]...Aggressive certainty replaces chaotic self-doubt...the power of fundamentalism is its capacity to interpret this reality even to those who doubt the core doctrines on which it is based.'[13] Unfortunately, these core doctrines include the Augustinian dogma on sexuality discussed in Chapter 2, as well as a literal interpretation of the Bible.

Interpretations of 'Irishness' on the British street

Failure to ground the differences outlined above arouses unease amongst Irish pro-choice activists who themselves may be fundamentally opposed to religious doctrine and to the Catholic and Protestant churches as institutions. Their experience is often that Irishness on the British street, and not infrequently in the British press and academy, is usually interpreted in fairly stereotypical and pejorative terms, such as 'Catholic', or worse, 'papist' (and 'nationalist', for which, read IRA) of the most atavistic kind. 'Papist' as a term of abuse in the British tradition has a long history rooted in its epic struggles with the Catholic powers of Europe, most of all with France. It is also rooted in the trumpeting of Protestantism as a superior ideology, where the exercise of the individual conscience is sacrosanct, where a personal relationship with the Almighty does not require transacting through the priesthood, and where allegiance is due to the monarch as head of the church, rather than to a foreigner ensconced in the Vatican.

When directed against the Irish, anti-Catholicism can also be taken as reference to a cultural pathology in which an entire people are cast as irrational followers of a religion which sees sex as sin. It is also a reference to unquestioning, even dumb, submission to authority in the person of a celibate divine in a black dress. While many an Irish 'joke' refers to Irish 'thickness' or stupidity, it is not unusual to find them tinged with a sexual or religious flavour, of the order of: 'Did you hear the one about the Irish rapist who tied his victim's legs together to stop her running away?'. Another which comes to mind is the limerick, 'Paddy is a moron – Spud thick Mick/Breeds like a rabbit – thinks with his prick/Anything floors him if he can't fight or drink it.'[14] It has to be remembered that for the period under discussion, the 1980s through to the end of 1990s, negative stereotyping of the Irish was at its height with British newspapers churning out an unrelenting diet of vicious anti-Irish cartoons and 'jokes'. One could be forgiven for thinking that these were far from being a matter of harmless fun, and were more likely devices being employed in Britain's war against 'Irish terror'.

Irishness, as much as Englishness or any other form of national identity, while not a meaningless or unusable concept, is generally regarded as one resting on shaky and questionable evidence and open to various shifts and shunts. In fact, there is nothing tangible, material, visible or fixed to define it absolutely. It is striking how rarely, if ever,

'Portuguese-ness' or 'Polishness' feature as a factor in discussions about reproductive rights – or the lack of them – elsewhere in the world. A notable exception, however, is the USA where cultural wars rage between liberals and fundamentalist Christians over the essence of 'American-ness'. This is especially true of the subject of abortion, and, of course, socialism and communism seen by many as decidedly 'unAmerican'. Where Irishness and reproductive rights are concerned, any debate on the subject in Britain is more or less guaranteed to bring forth quips about Catholics, convent girls, sexual repression and its spontaneous effect, namely, sexual incontinence, and the virgin/whore phenomenon.

In this context, it was with great interest that Irish pro-choice activists in Britain learnt of the long and intense debate in Mexico surrounding an appalling situation that eerily reflected the X case in Ireland in 1992. In this instance, the search for an essential 'Mexican-ness' did not seem to be a subject much debated in the media. In the Mexican case, the pregnancy resulting from the rape of 13-year old Paulina del Carmen Ramirez Jacinto by a heroin addict who broke into her home in 1999 was not terminated, contrary to the wishes of Paulina and her family. Unlike the Irish case where X was finally able to travel to Britain for a termination, Paulina was rebuffed by doctors at the Mexicali General Hospital. Their refusal to perform an abortion was not on legal grounds, since it is permitted in cases of rape in the state of Baja California. Rather, it was on the grounds of conscientious objection, pressure from the local Catholic hierarchy, and lay anti-choice activists.

By all accounts, debates in both the Mexican popular press and academic literature, and from the pro and anti-choice points of view, tended to present the case as a straight political fight. This contrasts with the Irish X case where essentialising Irishness became a major factor in debates in the British and foreign press. Even in Ireland itself it became an issue, as illustrated by President Mary Robinson's comment on the case in February 1992: 'I have this very real sense...that at the moment we are experiencing as a people a very deep crisis in ourselves'[15].

Amongst the few Mexican parallels was writer Carlos Monsivais'[16] reference to 'the collective discovery of horror' experienced by Mexicans over the Paulina tragedy. However, overall the power struggle graphically depicted in the media was less a psychological tussle of Mexicans with themselves. On the contrary, it was between the powerful institution of the Catholic Church, its adherents, particularly those in key positions in society, such as the medical profession, and the weak, but growing secularising tendencies in Mexico. These tendencies were reflected in the state of Baja California's relatively liberal law on abortion. Also seen as a major player was the dirty war being conducted in local and federal politics in which Paulina's case became a political football.

IWASG, an Irishwomen-only collective

It was in response to essentialism and the stereotyping of the Irish that IWASG became an Irishwomen-only collective from the beginning. The founder members' views were aired in an article penned by the group in *Feminist Review*, the British socialist-feminist journal, in 1988:

> *Over the years we've thought about opening the group to women who are not Irish but we've decided against doing this for political and practical reasons...We work closely with other [non-Irish] women who are interested in the issue and who are willing to provide the support we need...We work from the basis that we have a shared past, that we understand where women [abortion seekers] are coming from...*[17]

That anti-Irish racism was keenly felt is evident from the comments made during interviews with members. IWASG members were part of a widespread debate amongst the Irish in Britain, beginning in the 1980s. As Robbie McVeigh, who arrived in London in 1984 from Northern Ireland, explains, 'the notion of anti-Irish racism was born in struggle', and was far from being one 'discovered' by academics. Rather, 'it was named by Irish communities who had lived with its destructive consequences'.[18] Widely held amongst the Irish was the view that colour or visible difference – frequently cited as one of the key factors in the definition of racism – was inadequate as an explanation for what they encountered on a day to day basis.

Equally inadequate was the notion that *all* white people in Britain have control over power structures, a view held by many black and Asian commentators. By way of example, they saw the stereotyping of Irish people, not merely as bigotry, but as an act of disempowerment with a history stretching back to the twelfth century. This history was punctuated by key moments of Anglo-Irish conflict, whether the United Irishmen's rising of 1798 brutally squashed by the forces of the British crown, or the contemporary 'Troubles' in Northern Ireland. Like many Irish in Britain, IWASG members were perturbed by the unrelenting diet of vicious anti-Irish cartoons appearing in British newspapers throughout 'the Troubles' depicting the Irish as bestial or sub-human.

Annie Campbell, a member of IWASG, was one who explored the subject of anti-Irish racism in her interview. Annie had grown up in a Protestant and Loyalist working-class family in East Belfast where being British was a badge of pride. Her father had been in the British Army during the Second World War, and later was a B Special. He had also been a Transport and General Workers' Union shop steward.

Through some of the discussions in IWASG, and elsewhere, on issues about being Irish women in Britain, I began to work through the experience of anti-Irish racism – you didn't have to be there long before it hit you slap bang in the face. I suffered a culture shock when I was first treated as a 'Paddy', as someone belonging to the lower rungs of the food chain. It made me think about what it was to be Irish. Before that my background was influenced by my family's Britishness. My father's involvement in the trade union movement also influenced me where issues of class were concerned – there was a strong working-class tradition in the family.

Another thing was that I was estranged from people in Northern Ireland who saw themselves as Irish. In Belfast I'd never met Northern Catholic women, let alone women from over the Irish border. It was in London that I first met a woman from the Short Strand, a nationalist area that runs along the bottom of the road where I grew up. Also, I began to meet women from Donegal, Mayo and throughout the south. To me at the time they were like some sort of exotic species. It seemed to me that the reproductive rights issue brought us together and united us in a way that no other could.

Ann Hayes recounts how it was the level of discrimination being experience by Irish people under the Prevention of Terrorism Act, as well as anti-Irish sentiment in the society at large that caused her to join IWASG:

Besides helping Irish women, the other thing that made me want to get into activism is that up to the latter half of the 90s, Irish people in Britain were always under suspicion and many were harassed because of the Northern Irish situation, like what is happening to a worse extent now to Middle Eastern people and Asians since 9/11. As a young Southern Irish female I'd come across casual racism and prejudice in England. You'd be having a conversation with an Average Nobody, and suddenly they'd morph into a self-appointed authority and put me 'right' on what actually did happen in various periods of Irish history, etc., all of this history they presented as being gloriously 'Irish and irrational'.

This was all mild stuff in comparison to male Irish friends having to hear allusions to their violence/sexual dysfunction/terrorism/drinking. I was spared this on the basis of gender and possibly because of my Southern accent, implying gormless backwardness, rather than violent backwardness. Linked to the race generalisation there was often the Catholic girl or woman thing, again some self-appointed experts who still felt the need to pronounce – intriguing for them, tedious for anyone on the receiving end of such a monologue. Of course, similar gender distinctions are made in racist comments to black men and women, as well as Muslims, since these days the Irish are not the ones under the microscope.

Marian Larragy recalls that in 1981, when the hunger strikes were going on in the Maze Prison in Northern Ireland, she noticed that the Ann Summers sex shop on Tottenham Court Road in London's West End, had a display taking up the whole shop front window:

> *This consisted of a pyramid made entirely from mugs with the handles on the inside and the word 'Irish Mug' was printed on each. I think I saw something much later suggesting that the originator intended that this was a 'make love not war' type of statement. I remember that it impacted on me totally through the prism of Irish people being regarded as inept at everything, even sex.*

> *On the theme of sex and the Irish, I remember that Noreen Byrne told us at a meeting in London that she had visited a condom-making factory in England to get supplies for sale at the Well Woman Centre in Dublin where she worked. She told us she was regaled with a constant stream of stereotyping 'jokes' by the senior factory management for the duration of her visit. They must have realised they were talking to a potentially substantial buyer of their product. But somehow it seemed OK to them – till Noreen put them right! I think there is a great deal less of this now, partly because of the era of the Celtic Tiger and partly the ending of the war in the North.*

Mary Sexton, who emigrated from Northern Ireland in 1968, and got involved in IWASG in its early stages at the beginning of the 1980s, recalled how difficult it was to deal with the British media, especially at moments of high tension in Ireland over abortion issues, the X case in 1992 in particular. Mary remembers how journalists would 'ring us and more or less stipulate that we deliver up an Irish abortion seeker, the more depressed, oppressed, and suppressed the better. They wanted a "victim type". Not only were we unwilling to oblige, but it was IWASG's strict policy always to maintain confidentiality.' Mary also highlighted an aspect of the particular stresses and strains experienced by Irish abortion seekers as a result of 'the Troubles'. This related to the stereotyping of the Irish in Britain as a 'suspect community':

On top of all the other stresses and strains of coming to England for an abortion, for Irish women, there was the problem of state scrutiny and being seen as 'suspect'. Whether they came from Northern Ireland or the South, they were aware of surveillance at Irish and British air and sea ports. Measures put in place after the Prevention of Terrorism Act that came into play in 1974 resulted in surveillance of a new kind, the kind we have had to get used to since 9/11 and 7/7. Even in those days there were cameras located at strategic points. At Heathrow flights to and from Ireland were located at the far end of Terminal 1 for security reasons, it was said, and you had to walk half a mile or more to and fro.

All that piled on the pressure. You knew very well that every passenger was being closely inspected and monitored on camera as they progressed on their forced march, almost to and from the edge of the airport. You can imagine how nervous women coming for an abortion would feel. Even those of us not coming for that purpose felt hot under the collar. If you were heading back to Northern Ireland chances were that there would be further checks on the roads there by the British Army or the RUC and your details noted. Looking back, I suppose we just got used to it as long as we didn't get picked up.

CHAPTER 7

Introducing IWASG Women

Yet another crisis pregnancy: Ann's story

I remember my back-street abortion well. How could I forget? I've told my story many times, and more often than not, the response in Ireland and amongst the Irish in Britain has been an embarrassed silence. I suppose some find it prurient, likening it to a hunger striker or even a suicide bomber whose body is used as a political weapon. Less dramatically, some see it merely as a kind of attention-seeking ploy on my part; others just find it unbelievable. But it's all true. Looked at from the point of view of the many thousands, maybe even more, of Irish women who have aborted over the generations alive today, I'm normal. If numbers were what counted, we would surely be viewed as Everywoman, as normal as the girl next door.

I remember my abortion because in a funny kind of way it's been one of those life experiences that has made me what I am. The story is all too familiar. Girl meets boy. Both are lonely in a strange place. They fall in love and she gets pregnant. She panics and quickly falls out of love when he fails to understand her dilemma.

The details are a little more unusual. She was an Irish student cum-odd-jobber in London in the early 60s having fled an Ireland she rather grandiosely thought was too small for her. He was a Nigerian law student intent on returning home to do lofty things. He didn't see anything unusual in a teenager having a baby. After all, women in his family had several by that age, and he had offered to take her back to Nigeria to join them.

She liked the idea of travel, to Nigeria or beyond, but not to enlist in a very extended family. She wanted a life before babies. And what would her own family say about a black grandchild, whether in Nigeria or London? How would she provide for it? How would she and the child bear the stigma?

The story goes on. She cut herself off from the law student and began a search lasting months for an abortion in a London which was not yet swinging or even remotely liberal when it came to things like that. It was all too like Ireland, really. Finally, a friend-of-a-friend found a nightclub owner who knew about such things.

The abortionist was not quite the 'wise woman' of lore. She botched the job several times when the carbolic mix was either not strong enough or the rubber douche she employed failed to find its mark. She dreaded the return to the wise woman's dingy basement flat in sight of the Oval Cricket Ground in South London. She's never liked cricket since. Finally, the extra bars of Sunlight soap worked their alchemy and she returned to her bedsit alone to wait.

A massive haemorrhage resulted in her being whisked rather dramatically in a blaring ambulance to St. Mary's Outpatients in Praed Street, Paddington late that night. The young doctor was polite, just. He seemed keen to establish precise medical details she may or may not have supplied through the fog of pain which he said he could do nothing to alleviate. He did, however, follow legal procedure to the letter and had the police question her – unsuccessfully – about the abortionist. Those were the days before the 1967 Abortion Act.

On admission to a large ward full of women who seemed elderly to her youthful eyes, she was cordoned off in a curtained cubicle at the far end of the room and handed a bedpan on which she was told to sit. She sat and she laboured throughout an endless night, punctuated by her groans and the tut-tutting commentary of fellow patients whose gynaecological complaints must have seemed to them more acceptable than hers. She supposed she should have been grateful she was not put on the maternity ward, as she was later to learn had happened to others like her. Mouthfuls of bitten bed linen did something to muffle her intrusive noises.

Her early morning delivery coincided with the changing of a medical and nursing guard which informed her that she had to shower and then undergo an internal examination. Somehow she managed both. She was told she was suffering from septicaemia, a damaged uterus and considerable loss of blood. Worse, she was told that she had been a 'very silly girl'. She told them she had had enough and marched out like a drunken sailor to the strains of 'What do you expect of women like that?'

Looking back on the girl who tottered out of St. Mary's onto Praed Street that morning, I remember that I was too numb then to think of anything but immediate survival. In time, all the usual clichés about life never being the same again came true. I changed, I got angry, not at myself, but with the system. I spoke out, telling my story, saying 'the unsayable'. What I can say now, more than forty years on, is that for Irish women 'the unsayable' still needs to be said: women have abortions; abortion must be safe and legal.

Ann Rossiter

IWASG women – a miscellany of Irish life in London

This is my own abortion story which is closely connected with my reason for becoming an IWASG and Iasc woman:

I left Bruree, my home village in Co. Limerick, in my late teens in 1961 with only a Secondary School Leaving Certificate to my name and no skills of any kind, not even typing. The nuns at my school, the Convent of the Faithful Companions of Jesus in Bruff, Co. Limerick, never saw fit to give us career advice, feeling, no doubt, that it would be a waste of money for their pupils to pursue Higher Education or vocational training unless they were exceptionally bright or talented, like being good at music. Nothing much was said about what we might do after we left school, but it seemed to be accepted that any form of employment would be merely a stop gap until we married and became full-time wives and mothers. My parents were ambivalent, for even though I was an only child, money was in short supply to meet university fees and maintenance. So, I left seeking employment and adventure in England.

Predictably, I suppose, I became pregnant like so many Irish girls before me and after. The nuns and my parents had left me ill-equipped for life by a profoundly insular education and sexual ignorance. I have to laugh when I hear male commentators on Irish emigration matters saying that 'women are so much more able to cope with being immigrants than men'. If that means they are better able to cook a meal and wash their clothes, then they are right. As has been so often remarked, Irish mothers are renowned for leaving their sons incapable of dealing with an independent existence. However, what these male commentators forget is that adjusting to a world in which sexual relations are a lot more relaxed than they were at home, especially in the 1950s and 60s, coupled with the lack of sex education, the fallout for women can be devastating .

After my abortion I spent several years abroad during which I became a socialist-feminist activist, having been exposed to radical ideas and movements while living in France and Spain. I had helped Maria, one of my Spanish flatmates, to get a backstreet abortion while living in Madrid. I was young and didn't think of the consequences if we were found out by the authorities. Procuring an

140

abortion carried a tariff of life imprisonment under Franco.

Maria and I worked in the same bar and I found an abortionist through some American soldiers from a nearby US military base who frequented the place. Maria was unmarried, in her late 30s, and worn to a shred working round the clock to send money to her parents and many siblings in Andalucia. Her father had been in trouble with the police for his involvement in a farm workers' strike in one of the great southern quasi-feudal estates, or latafundia, as they were known. He never got work again.

Back in London in the early 1970s, I joined the British Women's Liberation Movement. I became involved in a number of campaigns, reproductive rights amongst them, hardly surprising given my own experience of a backstreet abortion in London before the 1967 Abortion Act was introduced, and my encounter with Maria in Madrid. However, the realisation that women in my own 'neck of the woods', the Republic, were still unable to access contraception (legalised as late as 1979 for married couples only), let alone a termination, led me to focus my attention on Ireland. As was common for many from the Republic, it came as a shock to learn that the situation was hardly different in Northern Ireland, designated a 'province' of the United Kingdom.

My abortion story, reproduced above, is a version of the one which first appeared in The Irish Journey: Women's Stories of Abortion, published in 2000 by the Irish Family Association under the pseudonym of 'Marie'. The use of a pseudonym was something I was very exercised about at the time, feeling as strongly as I do that disclosing the details of my abortion is about politics rather than aesthetics, and a strategy successfully adopted by women in France, Spain and Italy. However, I was persuaded by the editor, Sherie de Burgh, that all the other women contributing their stories wished to remain anonymous. I was left with the uncomfortable feeling, best expressed by

Sherie herself in the Preface to the book, that: 'Carrying a sense of shame for your country is a terrible burden.'[1]

My public acknowledgement, both in print and on television, of a backstreet abortion at the age of nineteen in London before the 1967 Act made a termination safe and legal, has been met, mostly with silence, but occasionally with an irritated remark, or two. These have been of the nature of, 'Do we have to know the gory details?', or, 'Is this level of detail really necessary?', or more trenchantly, 'This is almost pornographic! You are using the same shock tactics as the anti-choice lot waving foetuses in jam jars about.'

In the history of the Irish pro-choice movement, few women have been willing to speak openly about their experience, apart from a few exceptions, amongst them, the late June Levine, journalist and founder member of the Irish Women's Liberation Movement, the late Mary Holland, a journalist with the *Observer* newspaper,[2] and the singer, Sinead O'Connor, who publicly declared at the time of the X case that she had had two abortions.[3] The action of well-known French public figures, like the writer Simone de Beauvoir, and the actress Jeanne Moreau who, in 1971, signed a manifesto admitting they had had abortions in violation of the law, has never been replicated in Ireland, North or South, or even in the diaspora.[4] June Levine recalls in her book, *Sisters*, that Mary Holland had called upon Irish feminists to send their names to a list of women declaring they had had abortions that Holland herself headed. However, Levine recalls that the request was greeted with silence, including from Levine herself.[5]

The so-called 'contraceptive train', a day trip from Dublin to Belfast on 22nd May 1971, organised by Irish feminists working in the media to bring back scores of condoms and spermicides in defiance of the law,[6] and the visit of the Women on Waves ship to Dublin and Cork in 2001, described in Chapter 8, are probably the only Irish parallels there are to similar iconic moments in continental European history. These moments included the Italian feminist campaigns of 1972-5 when thousands of women descended on St. Peter's Square in Rome, shouting in the direction of the Vatican:

Tremate, tremate, le streghe sono tornate
Figli desiderati = figli amati
Tremble, tremble the witches are back
Wanted children = loved children[7]

They also included the *autoinculpaciones* (self-blame) campaign in the early to mid-1980s in Spain, when huge numbers of women across the country from different classes and positions in society declared: '*Yo tambien he abortado*' (I also have aborted). This had the effect of normalizing abortion at a time when doctors were being prosecuted for performing illegal operations. This campaign, and the action of doctors willing to flout the law, led to the *Cortez* (parliament) passing a law in 1984 legalizing abortion if the mother's life is endangered, in the case of rape, or in the case of a malformation of the foetus.

The way we were

The IWASG membership was distinguished by an array of different backgrounds and experiences in its ranks in terms of class, education, occupation and political belief. As already stated, their diverse occupations included bus conductresses, office workers and managers, IT specialists, nurses, pregnancy counsellors, social workers, voluntary (funded) sector workers, teachers and one or two academics. Various age groups were represented, as well as different sexual orientation. Some had been active in reproductive rights campaigning in Ireland itself before joining the group. There may well have been conflicting positions on 'the big issue' of the time, namely, the Irish National Question. Some IWASG women seemed openly sympathetic to Republicanism and were activists in one or more of the many different organisations campaigning on the subject, and some came from Unionist and Loyalist traditions which they may well have jettisoned along the way. The fact is that such views were rarely if ever promoted, or even publicly expressed in the group, for reasons that were possibly conscious as well as unconscious. Many of the Irish members of the group would have been acutely aware of the trouble and strife within Irish feminism in Ireland itself, north and south of the border, as an activist interviewed by Linda Connolly in her account of the southern women's movement attests:

> *...there were colossal arguments about the North. I mean, every single Sunday we would have an argument about the North...you had ones [women] that thought the North was very much part of our conflict...Then you had another section of women [who] felt that they didn't want anything to do with women in the North...They saw the history of women in the South as having been damaged by Republicanism.*[8]

In all likelihood, numbers of IWASG women were of a socialist, anarchist or libertarian persuasion which was as critical of Republicanism as of Unionism on the issue of reproductive rights. As far as religious belief was concerned, nobody ever declared an affiliation with the Catholic Church or with the various permutations of Protestantism, liberal or evangelical. Such issues were never a matter of debate or seeming concern in the group. In all probability it would be fair to say that most or all IWASG women were secular, possibly agnostic, maybe even atheist. Not everyone was pro-abortion, but all were pro-choice. What united them was their feminist belief in a woman's right to control her reproductive capacity. IWASG's sole criteria for membership were: support for the right of a woman to choose an abortion – or not – and that members be Irish or of Irish descent. In essence, IWASG was the classical single issue support-cum-pressure group or collective.

Amongst those active in reproductive rights issues in Ireland before coming to London was the photographer, Joanne O'Brien,[9] who had been a member of Irishwomen

United (IWU) in Dublin. IWU was founded in 1975 by activists with a background in socialist and radical politics. The group's interests and activities were diverse, from women and the trade unions to social welfare, but the most radical issue by far that they embraced was contraception, abortion still being a taboo subject in the Republic at the time. Joanne remembers her involvement in CAP (Contraceptive Action Programme) initiated by members of IWU in the late 1970s, a risky venture to say the least, given that as late as 1991, Richard Branson's Virgin Megastore in the centre of Dublin was pursued by the police for putting condoms on sale:

> *CAP set up a shop selling contraceptives on the South Circular Road in Dublin, all of which was illegal, of course. This was just before the enactment of the 1979 Health (Family Planning) Act which legalized the distribution and sale of contraceptives, but to married couples only. It would take another six years for the Irish government to legalize contraception for all those over the age of eighteen, married or single. There had been a stall in the Dandelion Market just off Stephen's Green, but it had closed down for reasons I can't remember. So we decided to open a shop.*

> *We'd got the premises very cheap and electricity was supplied for free by the man next door who had a photography-cum-chemist shop. He was a very nice bloke and he supported our cause. So, we painted the place, stocked it with condoms, and opened up. We advertised it around the town and on opening day we had RTE (the national radio and TV service) down. The first customer was a soldier from a local army barracks looking for condoms. Initially, I remember CAP members being worried that the business wouldn't take off, but it went like a bomb! So my joining IWASG was really a continuation of my involvement in Dublin.*

Another member of Irish Women United and the Contraceptive Action Programme in Dublin before she came to London was Marian Larragy. She says she joined IWASG, probably in 1981, when she heard about the group at a meeting at Turnpike Lane Women's Centre in North London. She recalls:

> *Irish Women United held a hugely oversubscribed public meeting on contraception at Liberty Hall in Dublin on the 12th November 1975. The advertising poster showed the profile of the middle section of a pregnant woman. The posters were put up everywhere there was an available surface round the city. Myself and a few others pasted one on the Daniel O'Connell monument near O'Connell Bridge. It stayed there for a long time, as the paper was thin and silk screen printed, and stuck like glue to Ireland's Liberator, its 'uncrowned monarch'.*

> *This success was followed by the setting up of CAP. We petitioned in Grafton Street in the heart of the city, but also in Ballymun flats, one of Dublin's poorest areas. While I was there I ran into a young mother who had been in my class in primary school. She signed the petition and told me that everybody in the flats was getting the pill 'to make their periods regular'. You only had to ask. She also told me that she had gone to a particular doctor to ask for help when she fell pregnant again just after the birth of her second child. She said that the doctor did not carry out a pregnancy test, but said he would refer her to the hospital for a D&C [dilation and curettage, or what was commonly known as 'a scrape']. She said that this was the usual thing to do if you thought you couldn't cope, although no one said anything openly. Those were the days before constitutional amendments and all that!*

> *At the same time, there were people in Galway who were sending contraceptives by post to anyone who asked for them. They were a collective of English men and women, and at least one of them was an IWASG supporter.*

Another IWASG member whose involvement in reproductive rights preceded her arrival in London was Pauline O'Hare from Northern Ireland.[10] She had been in the Northern Ireland Abortion Law Reform Association (NIALRA) in

Belfast since the time she was a university student. She recounts:

My reason for joining NIALRA was due to the experience of a friend who had had an abortion. I accompanied her to Liverpool and I remember that we were very frightened with the whole business of going to England in such circumstances. I remember phoning our parents from the docks and telling them that we couldn't go home that weekend, that we had to remain in Belfast to complete some extra homework and that we would see them the following weekend. We also took to lying to people on the boat when anyone asked us the purpose of our journey. The whole experience just increased the feeling that we were doing something wrong.

When we returned to Belfast I realised that abortion was such a taboo subject that my friend just wanted to put it behind her and we never spoke of it again. I could see over time how it affected her not being able to talk about it. If I had had any sense I would have broached it from time to time. But I was young and inexperienced. We stayed in a youth hostel in Liverpool, and there again we just peddled a load of lies. Why were there two of us on one night, and only one the second? I'm sure it was written all over us what we were about as loads of women in our situation must have passed through.

At Jordanstown [University of Ulster] where I was a student NIALRA members came to do a talk and have a debate. I was really enthused because this was the first time I'd experienced people standing up and talking about abortion in an open way. So I joined the organisation and started doing campaigning work. I was involved in the International Tribunal set up by NIALRA in October 1987 in helping to amass statistics and making arrangements for those sitting on the panel which, amongst others, included Wendy Savage from England, who at the time was a Senior Lecturer in Obstetrics and Gynaecology, Kadar Asmal, a law lecturer at Trinity

College, Dublin, President of the Irish Council of Civil Liberties and member of the African National Congress (ANC), Sarah Spencer, General Secretary of the National Council of Civil Liberties in Britain and Carol Tongue who was a Labour Party Member of the European Parliament.

I came to England in 1987 for a holiday but decided to stay. Mainly it was because of chronic unemployment in Northern Ireland – I had relatives there with a university degree who were working in record shops and the like and couldn't get anything better. When you arrived in London there was just so much work available. There was also a lifting of the weight of 'the Troubles', and I revelled in this sense of freedom, in the completely secular way of being that there is here. It was very liberating. I got involved initially with left-wing organisations in London, but I had difficulty with their thinking on the war.

I came across IWASG through the National Abortion Campaign (NAC) that I had contacted, but of course I already came to know them when they gave evidence at the 1987 NIALRA Tribunal. Although NAC was generally speaking supportive of Irish women's predicament, it didn't really seem to have much of an input in the Irish situation at either a political or practical level. IWASG was much more what I was about and, importantly for me, was not hidebound by dogma, and so I joined. Later, as well as working with IWASG, I became an abortion counsellor at the British Pregnancy Advisory Service (BPAS).

The experiences of Teresa Dunne,[11] a second-generation Irish woman, adds a further dimension to the web of Irish pro-choice activist stories:

My parents were immigrants, and at the bottom of the heap. They came over from Co. Limerick during the Second World War. My Dad had tuberculosis. We lived in London on a sink estate full of loads of people from different parts of the world. My parents hardly ever raised their heads above the parapet, so much so that I hardly knew I was Irish. I did go to a Catholic school and in the junior school there was Irish dancing, but in the secondary school there wasn't much that was Irish there. Another thing was that my parents rarely had enough money to go back home on holiday and maintain links with Ireland that way. In fact I was thirteen when I first went there with my Dad. My oldest sister never saw Ireland with my parents.

So, my parents' lives revolved around struggling to make ends meet. There was no space for taking up particular causes, like Irish republicanism, for instance, even though they were in favour of a united Ireland. Their way of dealing with things, I suppose, was to keep a very low profile in the face of a lot of anti-Irish feeling that started in the Second World War with the Free State (later to become the Republic) being neutral and De Valera refusing to let Churchill and the British Navy have the run of Irish ports. Then, of course, came 'the Troubles'. It's difficult for people like them to kick up about either their adopted or their home country, no matter whether it's about anti-Irish racism in Britain or the lack of women's reproductive rights in Ireland. They didn't discuss politics much. Of course, I'm not saying that people who are working class don't 'do' politics; far from it. It's just that when you're poor it's hard to find the space and time when work and family take up all your energy. For the second generation it's different.

I joined IWASG in either the late 1980s or the early 1990s. I saw a letter in Cosmopolitan asking for Irish women to join. I had had an abortion, I was of Irish parentage, had space in my house and I was single with time on my hands. So, a few boxes were ticked there and I thought I'd volunteer. I wasn't that politicised at the time. I didn't know much about political 'positions' on Ireland, but I learnt about it quickly. My job was in admin, so I thought I'd help out on minute-taking at meetings, keeping track of the finances (not that there was much of these) and the mail, and taking care of women coming over from Ireland. Mostly the women coming to stay with me went to St. Anne's Clinic in Tottenham.

Another second-generation Irish woman, Catherine Boyle,[12] outlines her reasons for joining:

I joined the group in 1992 when my son went to university at the age of eighteen. Also, of course, I had a spare room available to put women up. One of my reasons for joining was that I had my son when I was nineteen and I'd been given a choice about whether to continue with the pregnancy. I wouldn't say I am pro-abortion, but I'm certainly pro-choice.

My parents are working-class Irish and I was born, bred and have always lived in Kilburn (Ireland's 'thirty-third county') and I went to St. George's Catholic School in the Kilburn/Maida Vale borders. I feel very strongly, indeed, I feel very sorry for women in Ireland who don't have the same opportunities and choices on reproductive issues that women in Britain have, so I was glad to be able to help out with the work of the group. Also, I found that there was a great atmosphere there, a lot of camaraderie, a lot of committed and inspiring women.

Annie Campbell[13] from Northern Ireland was an IWASG member during her ten-year sojourn in London. Since her return to Northern Ireland, Annie has continued her involvement in the abortion issue. In Belfast, Annie became director of the Belfast Group of Citizens' Advice Bureaux, subsequently she was Vice-Chair of the Northern Ireland Anti-Poverty Network and is now Director of the Women's Aid Federation. She was a founder member of the Northern Ireland Women Into Politics community education project and a leading light in the Women's Coalition party, playing a key role in the talks process leading up to the Good Friday Agreement of 1998. Most recently, she was involved with the Alliance for Choice activism around the attempt to have the 1967 Abortion Act extended to Northern Ireland. Speaking of her experience with IWASG in London, Annie says:

My first encounter with politicised Irish women in London came about as a result of using the Kings Cross and Cromer Street Women's Centres in Central London and deciding to get involved in the Irish Women's Abortion Support Group in the early 1980s. It was in London that I came to identify strongly with the abortion issue. In fact, I was torn up by the thought of what women had to go through to get over [to Britain] and what I could do about it. For me IWASG brought together nicely the whole feminist analysis: if you don't have control over your fertility you don't have control over anything. Also, by being a member it meant doing something practical about it.

Ann Hayes, a voluntary sector worker who emigrated in the late 1980s, and who joined IWASG either in late 1994 or early 1995, says of her first encounter with the group:

I remember that I picked up an IWASG leaflet at an International Women's Day event at the Hackney Empire sometime in the '90s. Someone was going around distributing leaflets and looking for donations at the door as we filed out. I had the leaflet for a while and I thought I'll give this a try. I didn't know what it [IWASG] was really. I thought if there's a chance to do anything active, rather than belonging to a political party, I'll give it a try. About six months later I phoned the group.

I've never joined a party. I'm politically Left with libertarian leanings, but I don't want to spend time at meetings and committees. I'll go on demos and support campaigns, but politics is not my thing. At the time I wasn't well versed or interested in theoretical or ideological feminism. I just felt that abortion was something denied women in Ireland and maybe I myself would need one sometime, or my sister might need one. It was an equality thing rather than ideological feminism. I thought that this is a way of doing something to support Irish women but it doesn't mean going to committee meetings, meeting clergy, going to Irish centres where I

151

wouldn't be sure their agenda was purely for migrants' welfare, Irish dancing, the GAA (Gaelic Athletics Association), etc. I've absolutely no interest in any of that, and hadn't in Ireland either. All that being said, I identify myself as Irish, have interests in Irish culture, but want little to do with what I see as 'institutional culture'.

Explaining IWASG's credo and system of organisation

IWASG's political philosophy and organising principles were part and parcel of the counter-culture and libertarian currents of the time. It was decidedly feminist and probably there would have been wide agreement amongst all of those who passed through the group over the years on the following definition of a feminist:

> *...at the very least a feminist is someone who holds that women suffer discrimination because of their sex, that they have specific needs that remain negated, and that satisfaction of these needs would require a radical change (some would say a revolution even) in the social, political and economic order.*[14]

The idea of radical change involved a two-pronged approach: firstly, that there needed to be a re-evaluation of womanhood by women themselves through a process of 'consciousness-raising'. This meant a belief in the idea that women needed to translate their personal experiences which, until then, were seen as private and apolitical (e.g. pregnancy and childbirth, abortion, housework, straddling the divide between the world of work and maintaining a family, relations with men, domestic violence, sexuality, etc.) into political awareness and prominence. Secondly, it meant that there needed to be a practical programme of economic, legal and social reform. That the latter had been part of the first wave feminist movement stretching from the end of the nineteenth to the beginning of the twentieth centuries went without saying. It was the former – women voicing their own personal issues and concerns to the extent that 'the personal is political' became the central slogan of the second-wave movement – that was new.

As already pointed out, the group benefited from the input of a paid liaison worker, first at Release and subsequently at Women's Health and Reproductive Rights Information Centre (later to become Women's Health). However, IWASG's activities in general were conducted entirely on a voluntary and autonomous basis with decisions about the organisation made democratically at regular meetings. In line with feminist practices of the time, IWASG rejected what were seen as male-dominated, hierarchical and formal structures of 'Chairman', 'Deputy Chairman', 'Secretary' and Treasurer' in favour of relatively informal gatherings and the small group format.

Joan Neary points out, however, that despite its informal format, IWASG's business was conducted in an 'incredibly disciplined' manner. Meetings generally took place on a monthly basis, minutes were taken and unfailingly distributed to the full mailing list, including sister organisations in Ireland. Business matters consisted of arranging a rota for the oncoming month when a minimum of two IWASG women undertook to host, escort, and generally care for abortion seekers for the duration of their stay. A back-up person was usually chosen from the list of those members who offered accommodation only. Finances and fund-raising events were also discussed, the latter requiring considerable inputs of time, energy and ingenuity.

Other activities discussed and debated at the monthly meeting included the production of leaflets, posters and stickers for pasting on walls amongst the graffiti in public areas, such as toilet doors, trains and buses, to co-ordinate with pro-choice activists in Ireland who were also doing such work. Catherine Boyle remembers that one of the abortion seekers whom she looked after in London found out about IWASG in this way. She recalls that the woman, a 'Dub' living in the Northside of the metropolis, had noticed somewhat vaguely a London telephone number for Women's

Health in London saying something like: 'Pregnant and don't want to be, ring....', spray painted across a railway bridge on her street. She took little notice of it, as Catherine recounts, probably not beyond musing that for the graffiti artist to access such an awkward spot s/he had to be either totally drunk or OTT in her/his commitment to the cause. However, that changed when she found, to her consternation, that one day she was pregnant – and didn't want to be. Walking out of her door to see if the number was still there, she found to her surprise that it was still visible despite an unsuccessful attempt to efface it. Via this unusual method of communication, she made her way to London.

Then, there was the production of time-consuming items like the first handbook to become available containing details of abortion clinics in Britain, their location and transport connections, as well as their fees. The handbook was distributed free of charge to student unions and numerous pro-choice organisations throughout Ireland. Arrangements were also made concerning requests to participate in events, conferences and meetings held in Britain or in Ireland, as well as making contributions to publications. IWASG, for instance, was one of the organisations that gave evidence to the International Tribunal on Abortion organised by the Northern Ireland Abortion Law Reform Association held in Belfast in October, 1987 and referred to above by Pauline O'Hare.[15] In London in 1996, IWASG hosted a conference attended by representatives of a range of organisations in Ireland, including women's centres, rape crisis centres, women's refuges, and family planning organisations, to exchange information on the new, and much improved, situation developing in the Republic following the enactment of the Regulation of Information Act 1995 which allowed for details on accessing an abortion to be conveyed.

IWASG members also made a submission to the *Green Paper on Abortion* produced by the government of the Republic in 1999, the product of an Inter-Departmental Working Group on Abortion.[16] Although not included in its deliberations and ultimate publication, IWASG made representations to the group of feminist sociologists at Trinity College, Dublin researching for the publication, *Women and Crisis Pregnancy*,[17] commissioned by the Republic's Ministry for Health and Children and published in 1998 for inclusion of the services they provided. The case presented was that the Irish government should have a full picture of the abortion-seeking experience as witnessed by IWASG over nearly two decades.

There were also inputs to television programmes, examples being this author's discussion of her back-street abortion in the documentary *50,000 Secret Journeys*, produced by Picture House Company for *Radio Téléfís Éireann* (RTE), the Irish state broadcasting corporation, and finally shown after a censorship row on 20th October 1994, and in the British Channel 4 documentary *A Women's Fight to Choose* on 15th November 1997. Further to these activities, IWASG participated in a series of demonstrations outside the Irish Embassy in London at all of the key moments of reproductive rights recent history which have been described in the preceding pages. There were also occasional demonstrations outside the Irish Centre in Camden Town, notably when Gemma Hussey, member of Irish *Dail* (parliament), Minister of Education, and a spokeswoman on Women's Affairs, attended a St. Patrick's Day dinner at the Centre in 1983 (see photo on page 80) at the time of the constitutional amendment which placed the rights of the foetus on a par with those of the mother.

Sisterhood or feminist philanthropy?

Difficult, tricky and even traumatic situations apart, all IWASG women contacted in the preparation of this book evaluated their work in a positive light. Although political activity in IWASG waxed and waned, high points being in the early 1980s when the group was formed, and in the early 1990s when the abortion wars were at their height in the South, generally, they felt that theirs was a political as well as a practical contribution to progressive change in the area of reproductive rights on the island of Ireland. All of those interviewed mentioned their distaste for organisations that were mainly 'talking shops'; they were much more concerned to combine their politics with practical work, such as in IWASG. All pointed to the facility with which members worked together across class, ethno-religious (Protestant and Catholic), and political boundaries. Some questioned whether or not there should have been debate on the subject of difference, given that this form of transcendence could be taken as an unhealthy form of denial. It was suggested by some that there should have been more training to better deal with the medical and emotional complexities involved, while others felt these were areas for the professionals and that IWASG's work was merely about support.

Ann Hayes raised the thorny subject of a North-South Irish fund with contributions coming from either government or private sources, or both, to help women in difficult financial circumstances to have abortions. She queries why it is that abortion – and only abortion – falls outside free National Health Service provision in Northern Ireland. Other areas of National Health Service medical care are available to Northern Ireland residents should they find themselves in Britain and in need of treatment (this subject is discussed in more detail in Chapter 8). In fact, it is standard practice for doctors to refer patients requiring treatment unavailable in Northern Ireland to British hospitals. She says:

> At the back of your head you have the impression that you are bolstering a service that should be funded by the tax payer in Northern Ireland and the Republic. We are engaged in a version of philanthropy in the late twentieth and early twenty-first centuries, something that really belongs to the nineteenth century and earlier. This is all wrong, you think to yourself – it's a rescue mission or welfare feminism, if you like.

Ann also pointed out that while most abortion seekers were either self-referrals or provided with the information to access an abortion by organisations in Ireland, there were also 'under the counter' contacts made by state agencies in the Republic. On occasion, IWASG members received telephone calls from social workers and Health Board employees in the Republic requesting IWASG's help in referring women to clinics in Britain. Presumably, the abortion was being financed via official funds, and in Ann's words, 'Our guess was that the nature of this expenditure has never appeared on any expenses sheet. Had they not contacted us and gone through to the clinics directly they would, especially when the residency requirement was in place, have had to spend from public funds for accommodation. So in that way we have been able to help out the Southern Irish Exchequer!'

It may be that this practice has occurred on a more regular basis than IWASG members are aware, with Health Boards paying for abortions that are undocumented. Of course, it needs to be emphasised that the work of IWASG has also helped the British Exchequer by financially aiding Northern Irish women. Ann Hayes continues:

At times there was the assumption that we in IWASG were workers in some kind of non-governmental organisation (NGO) or other type of service, rather than voluntary activists. Usually this misunderstanding came from social workers in Ireland in the absence of any 'official' guidelines. I remember one abortion seeker politely asking me as we got on the Tube from the airport if I worked most evenings! When we got to my flat she was surprised to be given my spare room and an offer to share dinner with me. She had thought she was coming to some kind of institutional accommodation and that I was a paid employee. Perhaps we should look at this as a positive indication of how 'normalised' the service at this side of the Irish Sea must have started to appear to Irish social workers.

The problem of secrecy

When asked about the implications of maintaining secrecy, especially whether IWASG members should have been more proactive in publicising the existence of the group, and the reason why its services were required, Pauline O'Hare commented:

> To be honest, I can see why people both inside and outside of IWASG might have been impatient with us over the secrecy issue. I suppose it's very hard to understand it until you stand outside the situation and view it from a distance. There was collusion round the silence and secrecy issue on our part. Even when those of us in NIALRA were involved in the International Tribunal in Northern Ireland in 1987, we refused to appear on camera. There was a sense of fear, but when you think about it, what was this fear about?

> In 1992, when we were demonstrating outside the Irish Embassy in London over the X case, Sky Television turned up to interview us, and the pictures and interviews were relayed in Northern Ireland. People said to my Mum, 'Oh, we saw Pauline on the telly last night'. So it became public knowledge that I was doing campaigning work around the abortion issue. And the sun didn't fall out of the sky as a result of this being made public! What was the big issue, really?

> As far as publicly declaring ourselves, of course we have to remember that the IWASG banner appeared on virtually all the Irish marches and demonstrations, such as the yearly Bloody Sunday march, and there wasn't even a single complaint made by any of the participants, not ever, but then most of the marchers were socialists or republicans, or, more likely both. What you didn't see at these events were traditional Irish organisations, like the Federation of Irish Societies and the various Counties Associations, all of whom seemed to keep a low profile for the duration of 'the Troubles'. Despite our regular

presence, we weren't headline news in the *Irish Post.. For them we were that group of 'girls' who should be ignored.*

By rights, if we were really interested in publicising the issue more vigorously, we should have had the banner at feminist, trade union, and political events of all kinds, Irish and British, and pushed the issue like gays and lesbians did in New York when they insisted on being included on the St. Patrick's Day Parade, much to the chagrin of the Ancient Order of Hibernians.

Ann Hayes argues even more vociferously:

Because of the fraught nature of the abortion issue, no woman is going to go back to Ireland and say publicly, or to the health service, 'I'm angry because I had to get help or charity off a compatriot.' Nobody's done that so far, and chances are they're not going to do it ever because of all the secrecy stuff. People won't talk about this even though politically it's important that they do. It is the individual's absolute right not to talk about it. That we have to accept. But how long can this go on for?

Extend the '67 Act to Northern Ireland!
Diane Abbott MP (3rd from left) and Dawn Purvis MLA (4th from left) outside Parliament on 8th October 2008, organised by Alliance for Choice ©Joanne O'Brien

Iasc's first outing: Picket of London Irish Embassy, May 1990 organised by Women Against Fundamentalism. © Joanne O'Brien

CHAPTER 8

The Irish Abortion Solidarity Campaign (Iasc)

*'If you think you are too small to make a difference,
try getting into bed with a mosquito.'*
(Author unknown)

Iasc's last stand

On the 8th October 2008, a bright, sunny Autumn day, the rump of Iasc gathered outside the Houses of Parliament in Westminster. They were there making common cause with a symbolic group of Northern Irish women representing abortion seekers travelling each week to British clinics in an event organised by Alliance for Choice in Northern Ireland. The group was joined by Diane Abbott, MP and Dawn Purvis, MLA (member of the Northern Ireland legislative Assembly), and leader of the Progressive Unionist Party. The purpose of the gathering was to lobby MPs, but also to protest at what was beginning to look like a 'stitch-up' by the Labour government of Diane Abbott's proposed amendment to the Human Fertilisation and Embryology Bill calling for extension of the 1967 Act to Northern Ireland, due to be debated in parliament on the 22nd of the month.

The story behind the 'stitch-up' was an interesting one, as Goretti Horgan outlines in her Foreword. This stemmed from a letter sent in May 2008 to every Westminster MP, signed by the leaders of all of the main political parties represented at Stormont, from Unionists to nationalists and republicans, and the leaders of all the Northern Irish churches. The only exceptions were the Alliance Party and the Progressive Unionists, the latter being the only unequivocal pro-choice party in the Assembly. In their letter, the party leaders claimed to represent the views of ninety per cent of the Northern Irish population in rejecting extension of the Act, and, if that were not sufficient, they claimed that Westminster's dabbling in the affair would damage the Peace Process. Allegedly, the ultimate squashing of the amendment repaid a debt incurred to Unionists in May 2008, when votes from the Democratic Unionist Party saved the British government from defeat on proposals to allow detention of terrorist suspects for forty-two days without charge, a move which was ultimately defeated in the second chamber, the House of Lords.

Also being put forward in parliament were a few other amendments to the 1967 Act affecting women in Britain generally: one, calling for a single doctor instead of two to sign an agreement to terminate a pregnancy; two, nurses able to administer pills for early abortions; third, women be allowed to take these pills at a GP's surgery, rather than a clinic or hospital, to make the procedure quicker and cheaper. As Goretti Horgan[1] of Alliance for Choice in Derry recounts in her interview below, the Labour government allowed these and the Northern Ireland extension amendment to slip to the bottom of the list for debate on the day, with no time for discussion, as a result of the pressure from Northern Ireland Assembly leaders. Goretti says:

In 2008, it seemed that we were finally going to get equal rights for women in Northern Ireland. It was agreed by the Westminster government that the Human Fertilisation and Embryology Bill could be used to make amendments to the 1967 Abortion Act. Voice for Choice,[2] a Britain-wide coalition of pro-choice organisations, urged the All Party Parliamentary Pro-Choice and Sexual Health Group to include an amendment to extend the Act, finally, to Northern Ireland. It should be acknowledged that one of our great champions in parliament was Dr Evan Harris MP who, against all arguments, insisted that women in

Northern Ireland should have the right to all reproductive healthcare under the National Health Service.

In July, Emily Thornberry MP was to have put down an amendment on Northern Ireland, and her amendment was to be backed by a range of Labour MPs, including former Health Ministers, Patricia Hewitt and Frank Dobson. As women from Northern Ireland prepared to travel over for the debate, word came through that the amendment had not been tabled. Ms. Thornberry phoned Alliance for Choice to tell them that she could not 'put the Peace Process in danger' by going ahead with the amendment. In spite of our arguments that, far from dividing the political parties, they are all too united against women's right to abortion, she said she had to believe what Number 10 [the Prime Minister's office] was telling her about the dangers to the Peace Process.

Fortunately, Diane Abbott stepped in and put down the amendment and the debate was scheduled for some time in October. This gave Alliance for Choice the opportunity to intensify the campaign. A group was established in Belfast where a public meeting was attended by about one hundred and fifty people. Public meetings were also held in other parts of the North. None were disrupted by anti-abortionists and all brought together women and men who want to see the North enter the twentieth century [sic] in terms of attitudes to sexual freedom and the right to choose.

The amendment to extend the Abortion Act to Northern Ireland was not debated or voted on at Westminster because of a procedural motion put by Harriet Harman, Deputy Leader of the Labour Party, Leader of the House of Commons, Minister for Women and Lord Privy Seal, and supported by many New Labour 'feminist' MPs. This misguided political opportunism was a shocking act of betrayal of women by government ministers who have built their careers claiming support for women's rights. Harriet Harman had claimed that, were the vote to go *ahead, the House of Lords might reduce the current time limit for abortions. The facts do not bear this assertion out. House of Lords voting records show that the Lords have never reversed a House of Commons decision on abortion. In recent years, the Lords have voted for progressive positions eight times on embryo and abortion issues. The real reason the debate was not allowed to proceed was clearly due to other more sinister reasons.*

The notion that extending the Abortion Act to the North would put the Peace Process at risk, is nonsense. All four parties on the Executive are united against extension. How could extending the Act drive them apart? Support for extension, too, transcends the sectarian divide, and involves mobilising people on a basis which has nothing to do with whether they are Orange or Green. The basic Human Rights and Equality legislation introduced in Northern Ireland since the time of the Civil Rights movement has come from Westminster, why doesn't this also apply to women's rights?

After the failure to debate her amendment, Diane Abbott[3] wrote to Alliance for Choice to say:

As I said in my comments in the House today I did not table the amendment out of a desire to persuade people in Northern Ireland that abortion is a good thing. I did not table the amendment because I felt the need to override the authority of the Northern Ireland Assembly. And I did not table the amendment to force a single woman in Northern Ireland to have an abortion.

The situation as it stands in Northern Ireland means that this specific group of women are living in a country that has legalised access to abortion, but are excluded from this law. This specific group of women pay the same taxes as women in England, Wales and Scotland, but are not able to access the same services on the National Health Service. If I were to travel to Northern Ireland and break a leg, my medical treatment there would be free, but Northern Irish

164

women travelling to the rest of the UK for an abortion must pay. This is an inequality and an utter injustice.

Over the past months I have heard from hundreds of people on the issue of extending the Abortion Act to Northern Ireland. Overwhelmingly, these have been Northern Irish women, and some men, who have thanked me for giving women in Northern Ireland a chance at equality. The hundreds of people who have written to me and telephoned my office, the thousands of people who have protested and signed petitions, and the thousands more women whose voices have been silenced by a gap in legislation that does not recognise their rights as equal citizens of the United Kingdom nor their right to control their own bodies have today lost their chance to make their voice heard. Through a cynical and frankly undemocratic procedural motion, the Government today thwarted the chance to even debate the notion of extending the 1967 Act to Northern Ireland. Today the Government has let these people down.

I will be working with colleagues and the organisations who have worked so hard to inform Parliament about the need for access to abortion in Northern Ireland to explore what options we have now for bringing equality to Northern Irish women.

As a footnote to her comments above, on 28th January 2009, Diane Abbott tabled an Early Day Motion (EDM) in Westminster, calling on the government to 'provide funding for women in Northern Ireland to access NHS abortion services in Britain.'[4] The outcome of this EDM is awaited with apprehension amongst pro-choice activists on both sides of the Irish Sea.

In the beginning

Eighteen years before the Alliance for Choice demonstration outside parliament, the Solidarity Campaign, Iasc, emerged from another protest. That time, however, it took place outside the Embassy of the Republic of Ireland in London in May 1990 and was organised by Women Against Fundamentalism (WAF). The demonstration was in support for the Dublin Well Woman clinic and Open Line Counselling who were seeking to overturn a ruling by the Supreme Court in Dublin over the prohibition on abortion information.[5] WAF is a British feminist campaigning group which has had members of IWASG in its ranks. The group had been formed in 1989 at the height of the furore over Salman Rushdie's *Satanic Verses* and Ayatollah Khomeini's *fatwa*, and was the brainchild of Southall Black Sisters, a predominantly Asian advice and campaigning women's group with a centre in Southall, West London. WAF called for the separation of church and state (few at the time were aware of the confessional nature of the British state) as a basis for opposing fundamentalism, especially those aspects affecting women, not only in Islam, but in Christianity and all other religions.

The Irish Embassy picket was supported by IWASG, the London Irish Women's Centre and a number of other Irish and British feminist groups. It provided an outlet, as did similar protests throughout Ireland and worldwide, for Irish and non-Irish to demonstrate their distress and outrage at the situation in Ireland. Voices from India, Pakistan, Sri Lanka, the Middle East, from Britain and continental Europe joined Irish ones in chanting 'Not the church, not the state, women will decide their fate' outside the embassy in London. After the first picket, several others which followed were supported by Iasc, WAF, IWASG, the London Irish Women's Centre, Irish Women in Islington, Irish Women's Perspectives, Women and Ireland, Southall Black Sisters, the National Abortion Campaign (now Abortion Rights), the Irish in Britain Representation Group, and Socialist Alliance, amongst others, particularly during 1992 when the furore surrounding the X case in Ireland was at its height.

The decision to form a group dedicated to campaigning came about primarily because IWASG at the time had its hands full with support work as well as fund raising.

However, as indicated in some of the interviews with IWASG women, not all were enamoured of activism in the public arena, especially in the last decade of the group's existence. The subject of activism, together with that of secrecy (the abortion seeker's confidentiality apart), probably represented the only bone of contention in the entire history of the support group. Iasc had some overlapping membership with IWASG, and initially met at the National Abortion Campaign's (NAC) office at the Women's Centre in Wild Court in Holborn, Central London. The Women's Centre had a 'women only', policy, and when Iasc decided to include men and women in its membership, it moved the meeting venue to various sites. Iasc membership was also open to people of all nationalities.

As with IWASG, Iasc had the single political aim of supporting a woman's 'right to choose'. Similarly, Iasc was not dependent on funding from public or private sources, relying entirely on the commitment of those involved. The group directed its energies, not only on public protest (the last picket of the Irish Embassy was on 4th March 2002 on the eve of the fifth constitutional referendum on abortion in the Republic), but also on co-ordinating its activities with those pro-choice activists in Britain, such as Voice for Choice, the National Abortion Campaign, and in Ireland, the Alliance for Choice. An example of these actions was the 'fax-a-thon' on 17th June 1992 in which pro-choice groups in Ireland, Britain, the USA and elsewhere continuously faxed information sheets on abortion to public institutions and private businesses in the Republic, targeting those known to have a sizable female workforce. This date was chosen as a special day of action since it preceded the referendum on the Maastricht Treaty that included a protocol recognising the Republic's right to a constitutional ban on abortion within the European Union.[6]

Iasc members have also done extensive publicity work which has included giving seminar presentations, for example, at the Greater London Authority's Information Day on Irish women's health in May 2002, providing evidence at a conference convened by the Centre for Human Rights, Queen's University, Belfast for the international convention, CEDAW (Convention on the Elimination of all forms of Discrimination Against Women), on Northern Irish women's reproductive rights in April 2003, and addressing the National Union of Students' (NUS) Women's Conference in Blackpool in 2005. Group members have also published articles, including a lengthy piece in the *Irish Post*, the first time the newspaper had accepted a contribution, other than letters, from a British-based pro-choice organisation.[7]

Making waves with Women on Waves

Another example of Iasc activism was its involvement in 2001 with the organisation, Women on Waves, the brainchild of Rebecca Gomperts, a Dutch doctor who had a stint as resident medic on board Greenpeace's *Rainbow Warrior II* ship. As a result of her experiences in different parts of the world, Gomperts became concerned to act on the World Health Organisation's figure of 20 million of the 53 million abortions every year worldwide being conducted in unsafe and illegal conditions, resulting in 70,000 deaths annually as well as an untold number of medical complications.[8] Gomperts recalls: 'I remember meeting an 18-year-old girl in South America who was desperately trying to take care of her three younger brothers and sisters. She had recently lost her mother because of a back-street abortion. Her mother had been pregnant for the fifth time and couldn't support another child.'[9]

Women on Waves is a floating mobile medical facility which has so far sailed to many countries, including Ireland, Poland, Portugal and Ecuador, bringing a medical team, contraceptives, counselling facilities and information. It also has the aim of providing abortions on board ship while sailing in international waters (12 miles or more offshore where Dutch law applies to a ship registered in the Netherlands) to women otherwise unable to access safe abortion. Ireland was its first port of call, and after months of preparation (including the setting up of Women on Waves Ireland), and a multiplicity of hurdles, the Dutch ship, *Aurora* docked in Dublin Harbour on 14th June 2001 guided by the harbour police. On 22nd June it sailed to Cork Harbour where it was escorted by an Irish Navy ship and police boats. Its log records their preparations in Ireland prior to setting out on the June sailing from Holland:

May 2001

Many more people join the project, and Women on Waves Ireland grows into an organization with over 100 volunteers...Several well known artists and writers lend their names to the project and are among our earliest public supporters. For many of them, this is the first time they participate in abortion rights activities. More groups agree to support the ship's efforts. Some women's organizations, however, fear that by supporting us they will appear too strident on this issue. Since abortion is so controversial in Ireland, many who sympathize with our cause are hesitant to support us publicly due to concerns about their families and jobs [one young civil servant was suspended from his job because of participating].

May 19/22 2001

The [Irish] Feminist Majority Foundation, a group specialised in clinic defence, trains volunteers in Cork and Dublin on security issues and procedures. This training prepares us to deal with a variety of scenarios such as bomb threats, large scale protests and individuals disrupting programs. We do not know what to expect.

It appears that extremist American anti-abortion groups such as Operation Rescue trained the Irish Youth Defence, an aggressive anti-abortion group. Furthermore, the murderer of Dr. Slepian, an American doctor who performed abortions [in the U.S.], has found refuge in Ireland for over a year.

We have been very fortunate to find an anonymous private donor to cover the entire cost of the professional security.[10]

Having been led to expect a reluctance on the part of Irish women to come on board in the face of a global media frenzy and a barrage of anti-choice protestors (a Catholic bishop sailed his boat in a protest demonstration around the harbour), the opposite was true. The ship was inundated with those seeking information and terminations, including women from Afghanistan, Nigeria, Romania and the Ukraine resident in Ireland, some of whom were refugees and unable to get permits to travel to Britain for abortions, or found that the necessary paperwork for exit visas was delayed through government bureaucracy. Although the 'morning after' pill was available on board the *Aurora*, legal complications in Holland and in Ireland prevented abortions being performed.

There were hundreds of telephone calls from around Ireland, North and South from women with unwanted pregnancies who were unable to get to the boat. Some were from women who were raped, one from a fifteen-year old schoolgirl who had been thrown out by her family because she was pregnant, others were from refugees who did not have the papers to leave the country. Many of the women were diverted to Iasc in London where the group organised a 24-hour emergency answering service providing information on clinics. As much money as could be mustered at short notice on both sides of the Irish Sea was made available to women who wished to travel to Britain to have a termination, but were short of funds.

Despite the bomb threats, the suspicious underwater activities around the boat, and the sporadic, but often minor forays of anti-choice activists, such as the sprinkling of holy water over the ship, Juliet, a doctor from the Irish organisation, Doctors for Choice, recounted that after the ship's visit, 'The public mood has shifted in the past months, mainly thanks to the Women on Waves project – it normalised everything. Women are now phoning up radio programmes speaking about their abortion experiences,

170

which was unheard of before! The press is generally pro-choice, in particular the *Irish Times*. The Labour Party has openly declared itself to be pro-choice, the first [parliamentary party] in Irish history'.[11]

Gomperts argues that although no abortions were performed on the *Aurora* during its Irish trip, Women on Waves' tactic of direct action was a very visual challenge to the status quo. Various workshops were held on board to discuss legal and medical issues relating to the Irish situation. An artists' workshop, as well as a writers' workshop displayed and discussed their work, addressing issues such as fertility, sexuality and human rights. In fact, many Irish feminist activists pointed out that nothing so dramatic had occurred since forty-seven members of the Irish Women's Liberation Movement took the 'Contraceptive Train' from Dublin to Belfast and back, illegally importing contraceptives into the Republic in May 1971. In the process, an international press furore was created and a national conversation on the topic of contraception was initiated. After their sojourn in Ireland, Women on Waves went on to sail to Portugal in 2004 where they were blockaded by two war ships, thereby raising a hue and cry in the country, all of which contributed to abortion becoming a focal point in the 2005 election.[12]

The survey, *The Other Irish Journey*

As one of many attempts to break the silence, and to bring home the reality of abortion as a fact of daily life in Northern Ireland, Ann Rossiter and Mary Sexton of Iasc undertook a survey of Northern Irish women attending the clinics of Marie Stopes International in London in the period September 2000 to March 2001. A number of women attending the Northern Ireland Family Planning Association in Belfast for pre-abortion counselling were also surveyed. The idea for the survey, *The Other Irish Journey*, came about at a meeting of the All-Party Pro-Choice Group at the House of Commons sometime in early 2000 and was subsequently supported by Voice for Choice, both of which have a policy of extending the 1967 Act to Northern Ireland.

The decision to focus on Northern Irish abortion seekers exclusively was twofold. One reason was that responsibility for abortion legislation in Northern Ireland was vested in the Westminster parliament, a situation which also applies to Wales, and to Scotland, although the latter has its own legal system. The second reason was that criminal justice matters, including abortion, are to be devolved to the Northern Ireland Assembly, after which time the extension of the 1967 Act would no longer be an option. At the time of writing (January 2009), it is estimated that such powers are likely to be devolved in October 2009, although this is not certain.

With its argument in favour of extending the Act, the survey was seen by its authors as a contribution to the work of pro-choice activists in Northern Ireland committed to extension of the legislation before devolution of criminal matters takes place. Once that occurs, any abortion law emanating from the Assembly is likely to be highly restrictive, thereby setting in motion once again the flight of Northern women to British clinics. They were also concerned to debate the issue of Northern Irish women accessing abortions free under the National Health Service, a key recommendation of the survey.

Launching the survey: stranger than fiction

The Other Irish Journey was launched in Stormont, the Northern Ireland seat of government, on 30th October 2001, sponsored by Jane Morrice, Member of the Legislative Assembly (MLA) of the Northern Irish political party, the Women's Coalition, and the late David Ervine MLA of the Progressive Unionist Party. A further launch took place at the House of Lords at Westminster on 1st November 2001, sponsored by the All-Party Pro-Choice group and chaired by Baroness Gould.

When Audrey Simpson, Director of the Northern Ireland Family Planning Association, first suggested the possibility of a Stormont launch, the spectre of the institution as the embodiment of the 'Protestant state for a Protestant people' loomed large in the minds of the survey's two authors. Even the building itself indicates a place apart. Set at the end of a magnificent driveway, its Greek classical style and Portland stone façade are reminiscent of the U.S. Capitol in Washington D.C. No place, one might say, for the plain people of Ireland. And certainly not the natural stomping ground of the two Iasc women, both ex-Catholics, one from Sion Mills in the North, the other from Co. Limerick in the South. In dramatic pose in the sweeping driveway is the statue of Edward Carson, a Protestant lawyer from Dublin. Carson's chief claim to fame was his prosecution of Oscar Wilde, and his passionate opposition to Home Rule in the early part of the twentieth century. The imposing edifice of Stormont and its statuary serve to ram home the relationship of Stormont to Unionist rule to the British imperial connection.

The launch took place in the elegant Long Gallery at Stormont where an audience of about fifty representatives from organisations ranging across a wide spectrum of health, social and political fields, and some, like social workers and health care professionals, directly concerned with women's reproductive well-being. Others, like Alliance for Choice, were more involved in reproductive choice campaigning. There was also strong representation from the press and articles, all of them surprisingly positive, appeared in the *Belfast Telegraph*, *Belfast News*, *Women's News*, *The Irish Times* and *Nursing Times*, and there were broadcasts on Ulster Television's evening and late night news, BBC Radio Belfast and Downtown Radio. It was clear that it was not only the subject matter that was attracting attention, but the audacity and novelty of the launch at Stormont. As well as the Iasc authors, the event was addressed by Helen Axby of Marie Stopes International, Dawn Purvis (now leader) of the Progressive Unionist Party, Elizabeth Byrne McCullough and Audrey Simpson, both from the Family Planning Association.

Distinguished by their absence were representatives from the main political parties, viz., the Ulster Unionist Party, the Democratic Unionist Party, Sinn Fein and the Social and Democratic Labour Party. Although the Alliance Party had declined to sponsor the launch following lengthy discussions with the authors, a party member made a welcome and constructive contribution to the debate. Strains of distant chanting formed a backdrop to the proceeding as about twenty-five members of the anti-abortion group, Precious Life, staged a two-hour protest dressed in Halloween costumes and holding placards saying: 'Marie Stopes International kills babies.' The protest served as a reminder of the extent and zeal of the opposition, bearing in mind that only four months earlier, in June 2001, one of the first acts of the newly-convened Northern Irish Assembly was the rejection by a majority vote of extension of the 1967 British Abortion Act. This move was supported by the main Unionist parties, and by the Social and Democratic Labour Party and Sinn Fein on the nationalist and republican side. It also served to underline the question of whether, despite all the drama, symbolism and cachet involved in bagging Stormont and the House of Lords at Westminster as launch pads, the one-year slog of research, launching and publicising the survey was worth the effort involved, given the panoply of the parliamentary forces ranged against.

Feeding into such doubts was a disheartening meeting that had taken place with a young female Sinn Fein MLA at her Stormont office to discuss the launch of the survey, and which had elicited the response: 'Abortion is not an issue here in Northern Ireland'. She seemed completely unruffled at the response: 'So much for the thousands of women who have travelled to England for a termination since the introduction of the 1967 Act, including members and supporters of your own party', from the authors. 'In any case', the MLA continued, 'the party would not be in favour of extending the British Act'. Presumably, this was a reference to Sinn Fein's opposition to British, rather than home-grown, abortion legislation being introduced.

This point was later reiterated by a Sinn Fein councillor, Eoin O'Broin, in his office at Belfast City Hall. He agreed that legislation generated from within the Assembly was the preferred option. Also, he confirmed that the party's existing position on abortion, although ambiguous, was more or less in line with the existing legislation dating back to 1861. This allowed for abortion where a woman's life was in danger, and in the case of rape or sexual abuse. Suffice to say that Sinn Fein's opposition does not extend to a range of other British legislation, stretching from economic issues to education, health, and welfare. Goretti Horgan of Alliance for Choice in Derry, comments on the double standards involved in resistance to the extension of the 1967 Act:

There has long been controversy amongst pro-choice people in the North about whether we should look for the extension of a British act or not. By 1995 as the Peace Process got underway and the business of devolved government was being debated in detail, that the whole argument about not wanting British laws began to unravel. It began to show up as just camouflage – a cover – for not really supporting a woman's right to choose. If you look at the unfolding of political matters at the time, you will see that the British government was being looked to by Northern Irish politicians on both sides of the divide as an honest broker even within the Peace Process. There wasn't any problem about importing Westminster laws, lock, stock and barrel, in general. It was just abortion that was a problem for them.[13]

When first approached, the Women's Coalition did not dismiss the idea of sponsorship out of hand, but initially was uncertain about taking a radical stance on reproductive choice, as the party's manifesto spoke only of a commitment 'to working for a situation where women have greater control over their lives, so fewer women are faced with an unwanted pregnancy.'[14] Launched in 1996, the Women's Coalition was the product of frustration amongst Northern Irish feminists across the two communities over the stagnation of local politics, and also the practice of existing political parties in marginalizing women and women's issues. The party played an important role in the talks process leading up to the Good Friday Agreement of 1998, and two of its members were subsequently elected to the new Northern Ireland Assembly although they lost their seats in the Assembly elections of 2003. The party was finally wound down in May 2006.

Despite initial hesitation, on-going discussions within the Women's Coalition over developing a reproductive rights policy dovetailed with Iasc's request for sponsorship. This ensured that *The Other Irish Journey* got its day in the sun at Stormont. Although the sponsorship episode was hardly a defining moment in the Coalition's reproductive rights policy formation, it certainly can be seen as giving it a nudge in the right direction. The conclusion of the affair was that Progressive Unionist Party (which agreed with alacrity), together with the Coalition, sponsored the survey (Assembly rules dictate that the support of at least one party is required), and endorsed its call for extension of the 1967 British Abortion Act to Northern Ireland.

Unlikely bedfellows

Doing political business with sister feminists in the Northern Ireland Women's Coalition was all of a piece for Iasc, engaging with the Progressive Unionist Party was an altogether different kettle of fish and led to moments, if not of torment, at least of distinct unease, even queasiness. This was in spite of the atmosphere of the 'new' Northern Ireland in the making that followed the Good Friday Agreement where the past was meant to be dismissed as 'another country' and close working with former sworn enemies was the order of the day. However, rubbing shoulders with the political representatives of former Loyalist paramilitary organisations was a novel experience, to say the least.

The Progressive Unionist Party had emerged from the Ulster Volunteer Force and the Red Hand Commandos, the latter seen as no better than a Loyalist murder squad, having instigated a string of atrocities, including a tit-for-tat killing of, first two Catholics in a pub in the New Lodge district of Belfast, followed by six Catholics in a bar in the Short Strand area in 1975.[15] Their supposed founder John McKeague, ultimately assassinated by the IRA, was acquitted in a Belfast court in 1982, having been charged under the Religious Hatred legislation. McKeague[16] had published an 'Orange Songbook' which contained lyrics such as:

If guns were made for shooting,
Then skulls were made to crack.
You've never seen a better Taig[17]
Than with a bullet in his back.

The Ulster Volunteer Force, the most important component of the Progressive Unionists' forebears, had been first formed by Edward Carson in 1913 as a para-military bulwark against Home Rule in Ireland. Although officially disbanded with the emergence of the Northern Ireland statelet in 1920, it continued to have shadowy existence and provided a continuous supply of members to the Ulster Special Constabulary, popularly known as 'the Specials', an overwhelmingly Protestant militia and the bane of the Catholic population, which was disbanded in 1970 and replaced by the Ulster Defence Regiment. The Ulster Volunteer Force reappeared on the political scene in the mid-1960s, becoming engaged in a spate of random sectarian murders of Catholics instigated in the belief that a republican conspiracy was afoot to overthrow the Northern Ireland government and install the Pope as ruler of all Ireland.

However, it was for its opposition to the 1973 Sunningdale Agreement, the power-sharing (Catholics and Protestants jointly) devolved administration at Stormont proposed by the British government between Unionism and the 'moderate' nationalists, the Social and Democratic Labour Party, that the Volunteers are best remembered. Together with Ian Paisley's Democratic Unionists and other Loyalist factions, such as the Ulster Defence Association, a general strike was called in May 1974 which brought Northern Ireland to a standstill and put paid to notions of power-sharing.[18] Following the Good Friday Agreement of 1998 and the formation of the new Northern Ireland Assembly, the Progressive Unionists came to be represented in Stormont, and alone amongst Loyalist and Unionist political parties showed concern for reproductive rights. The late David Ervine's comment at the launch was instructive for both its attention to women's rights and its emphasis on the British connection to Northern Ireland:

> *It is a disgrace that in an alleged modern society such as the United Kingdom, women in this region are not being afforded equal citizenship. While we have much to do in Northern Ireland, including removing the stigma surrounding abortion and creating an atmosphere conducive to rational debate, our counterparts at Westminster must ensure that women's health in Northern Ireland is given the same importance as it is in London or Liverpool. To this end, Westminster must extend the 1967 Act and provide funding to Northern Irish women in the interim.*[19]

Promoting the survey

One of the main aspirations Iasc had in the promotion of *The Other Irish Journey* was to reach out to the burgeoning women's community sector in Northern Ireland. This idea was mooted at the launch at Stormont and seemed to gain approval of the audience. Mary Paul Keene, a community education worker and researcher in the field, has estimated that at least around a thousand community-based education organisations were set up by women throughout the island of Ireland 'seeking to address their own needs and the needs of their communities'[20] in the mid-1990s to the early 2000s, although many were short-lived due to lack of funding. The historian, Myrtle Hill, estimates that around four hundred of these have been based in Northern Ireland, 'in nationalist, unionist, urban and rural areas', with most groups 'working within their own locality, securing "peace" funding to run classes on health, politics, local environmental issues, history and creative writing'.[21] Taking into account that each community group may well have been catering to between fifty and one hundred and fifty women annually in a total (male and female) population in Northern Ireland of one and three-quarter million, it can be safely said that a significant number of adult females have been touched directly or indirectly by this phenomenon.

To this end, Iasc contacted approximately three hundred women's organisations, as well as trade unions with a predominantly female membership, community centres and health-related institutions in the period from November to Christmas 2001, offering to discuss the survey and its findings with audiences, small or large. The authors were confident that because of its interviews with abortion seekers, and its exploration of Northern Irish women's practical needs and problems regarding their journey to and from the clinic being presented in some detail, the survey was not a 'run of the mill' piece of statistical work. Thanks to a grant from the Simon Population Fund based in London, a small pot of money was available to cover travel and expenses for a few trips to Northern Ireland. The aim was to link the survey findings to the authors' experiences of doing abortion support work, as opposed to approaching the subject from an academic or researcher point of view. It was also felt that as well as being pro-choice activists, the authors were 'insiders', both being Irish, and in tune with Northern Irish women's practical needs as abortion seekers.

Unfortunately, the response was far from encouraging and led to some heavy soul-searching and self-criticism in Iasc. No matter how carefully it might be written and presented on paper with a broad audience in mind, it was not sufficient, it seemed, to write a report or to conduct a survey on the back of a wave of anger and distress experienced every time a Northern Irish abortion seeker sits at a kitchen table in London pouring her heart out. A play, or a even a documentary film on the Irish abortion experience, like

Melissa Thompson's *Like A Ship in the Night*,[22] might have been much more appropriate.

There were two important factors that Iasc missed by a long chalk in their failure to reach out to audiences. One of these was the extent of war weariness the society was experiencing in general after decades of bitter division and strife. Many local activists, including Annie Campbell from the Women's Coalition, suggested that abortion is such a highly divisive subject in Northern Ireland that even ardent pro-choice activists were finding it hard to muster the energy for a high profile and concerted abortion campaign, especially in the early 2000s, only a few years after the Good Friday Agreement was signed. The second factor was the rise of women's groups in the community sector and the exclusion of the abortion issue from their agendas.

There has been much comment on the role women's groups have played in Northern Ireland over the course of thirty years of war and its aftermath.[23] Some of these groups were distinctly feminist in orientation, and they operated either partially or wholly on a voluntary basis. There was the Northern Ireland Women's Rights Movement (NIWRM), the Socialist Women's Group and the Belfast Women's Collective, all of which emerged in the 1970s and campaigned for social and economic equality and for reproductive rights. Specifically geared towards work on reproductive rights were the Northern Ireland Abortion Law Reform Association (NIALRA) and its successors, the Women's Right to Choose Group, followed by Alliance for Choice.

These groups are distinct from the Family Planning Association and the Brook Advisory Service which are funded charities. They are also distinct from women's centres, the first being the Belfast Women's Advice Centre opened in 1979, followed by others opened in the 1980s and 1990s. Some are located in working-class areas, and in both Catholic and Protestant communities. They are a departure from the non-funded, voluntary groups in that they are grant-aided and have paid employees. However, they have retained a feminist agenda, being concerned to offer help and advice on a range of issues from domestic violence and abortion, to education and training for women entering the workforce and updating their skills. In fact, IWASG has had numerous calls from these centres requesting help for women coming over to London for terminations. However, the burgeoning women's community group sector was of a different order, and this difference may go some way to explain the negative response received by Iasc.

Women's community groups – feminist or familist?

Following the 1994 Republican and Loyalist cease-fires and the signing of the Good Friday/Belfast Agreement in 1998, considerable amounts of funding were made available to organisations aimed at promoting peace, reconciliation, social engagement, and the regeneration of civil society within Northern Ireland. The funding came from a variety of sources, amongst them the British government, the European Union, and the International Fund for Ireland.[24] A considerable slice of this funding was targeted at women, presumably in the belief that as a gender they are somehow able to transcend the ethno-religious divisions that have corroded civic and political life in Northern Ireland since its inception. Some, such as the community worker and researcher, Mary Paul Keane, have been enthusiastic about such developments. Others, such the historian and academic Myrtle Hill writing in her book, *Women in Ireland: a century of change*, seems to be more circumspect, suggesting that women's community groups could be either feminist or 'familist' (by this she probably means 'family oriented', such as the Women's Institute in Britain or the Irish Countrywomen's Association in the Republic) in their composition and objectives.[25]

Hill argues that the work of these local groups has often provided a gleam of light during the difficult times following the cessation of hostilities in Northern Ireland. She also highlights an important point, which is that on both sides of the border these groups were a lifeline for rural women, or those living in small towns where facilities were limited or non-existent, as well as in working-class inner city neighbourhoods. As such, these have proved to be important for social networking, and because of the educational and vocational training on offer, they were routes to the workplace.

Assessing the relationship between the community groups and the feminist movement in the Republic of Ireland (also applicable to their Northern Irish counterparts), Eilis Ward and Orla O'Donovan are more critical. They suggest that although the groups' existence has been lauded as an example of the vibrancy of the Irish women's movement, their impact was primarily on women's personal and private lives, rather than on raising a feminist awareness of issues, such as reproductive rights. Abortion, they say, was deemed 'too political' for attention by many members of the groups. In essence, Ward and O'Donovan argue that such groups can have a de-radicalising effect through their emphasis on the building of interpersonal relationships, while discouraging a feminist consciousness and a feminist practice, especially where women's traditional role in the family is concerned. They also suffer the negative impact of being funded and the forced bureaucratic demands of accounting, organisational regulation, and goal setting. It is clear, they say, that 'these groups do not necessarily a women's movement make.'[26]

By way of conclusion

Questions still surround the possibility of extending the 1967 Act to Northern Ireland in the wake of the debacle over the amendment to the Human Fertilisation and Embryology Bill. As has been outlined at the beginning of this chapter, there has been considerable movement forward on the ground in Northern Ireland in recent months. There has been the expansion of Alliance for Choice whose website buzzes with information on meetings, demonstrations, pickets, etc. There has been a declaration of support for the extension of the 1967 Act by all of Northern Ireland's largest unions: UNITE, UNISON, NIPSA, and many of the smaller unions (several of these displayed their banners on the protest outside the Westminster parliament on 8th October 2008). Further, there are the initiatives of the Family Planning Association in Northern Ireland, not least initiating a petition calling on the Prime Minister to reconsider extension of the Act. The Family Planning Association in Britain has also been active on the subject, as well as Voice for Choice, the All-Party Pro-Choice and Sexual Health Group, and the endeavours of MPs, Diane Abbott and Evan Harris, in particular. Most importantly, there is serious questioning ongoing of the claims of the politicians and church leaders to represent the views of ninety per cent of the population of Northern Ireland regarding the extension of the Act. As a letter to all British MPs states, 'there having been no test of public opinion and evidence from civil society'[27] to that effect.

Nationalising 'those bellies!'

On the question of Northern Irish politicians of disparate, even polar opposite political opinions, finding common cause in the prohibition of reproductive rights, it is the case that the phenomenon has parallels in contemporary Europe. In fact, it has been a remarkable feature of the transition of Eastern European states from communism to democracy. As Yudit Kiss, the Hungarian writer has put it:

> It is rather telling that one of the first big discussions of the newly elected [Hungarian] parliament took place about a draft law to ban abortion. It is rather intriguing that in the middle of a deep economic crisis, political chaos and social insecurity, when the foundations of society are to be reshaped, abortion has become a primary question in almost all post-socialist societies.[28]

Peggy Watson,[29] a Cambridge University academic researching the subject, relates that a member of the Polish Senate claimed that the reason for concentrating on the abortion issue at the expense of other pressing problems 'was simply because it was regarded as something that *could* be done'. By this he meant that the regulation of women was an area where 'power could be readily exercised, whereas the economy engendered feelings of powerlessness'. Another Polish Senator was heard to exclaim, 'We will nationalise those bellies!' Watson argues that legislating against the right to abortion serves to institutionalise the power of men. In Poland, in particular, there is also the fact that the Catholic Church carries much political clout and its sponsorship is crucially important for political parties. Watson also points out that in Eastern Europe relegating women to the domestic sphere smacks of a radical re-ordering of society, taking into account that women in these societies have had an unbroken record of working outside the home for nigh on half a century – that is, until 'democracy' arrived.

The invention of a 'new' social order is nothing new on the island of Ireland either. South of the border, a state born in violence, and divided by bitter quarrels, pursued a national identity through the imposition of a remarkable degree of conservatism and incorporation of the tenets of the Catholic Church. Since then, lessons learnt over nearly nine decades show the struggle to reverse this order of things can be rough as well as lengthy.

Listening to young Northern Irish students and to union members who joined the protest in Parliament Square at Westminster on the 8th October 2008, it became clear things may well be different in Northern Ireland. None of these young women were willing to accept the 'new' Northern Ireland forged according to the tenets of fundamentalist Protestantism and conservative Catholicism. What was particularly interesting was that not all would have called themselves feminist, but all were passionately pro-choice, a point illuminated by the following observation:

> *Part of the legacy of... feminism is that young women today have available to them ideas not only about being able to make choices but that the very notion of choice is their fundamental right. That they do not acknowledge*

their debt to feminism is an indication of the extent to which feminism in late modernity is not a marginalised discourse but has become a basic part of the context in which young women are making sense of their lives.[30]

'The Future', two young Northern Ireland women picketing
Parliament on 8th October 2008   © Joanne O'Brien

LIST OF INTERVIEWEES

Gautam Appa, 10/3/2008
Angie Birtill, 28/1/2008
Brid Boland, written communication, 12/8/2008
Catherine Boyle, 12/1/2008
Noreen Byrne, 29/10/2007
Annie Campbell, 8/10/2004
Kate Duke, 10/1/2008
Teresa Dunne, 2/1/2008
Blanca Fernandez, 21/2/2008
Goretti Horgan, 27/11/2008
Ann Hayes, 12/11/2007
Marian Larragy, email correspondence, 5/1/2009
Isabel Ros Lopez, 20/11/2007
Iris Lyle, 27/10/2007
Brian McCarthy, 3/2/2008
Ellen Mullin, 24/10/2008
Joan Neary, 2/10/2007
Joanne O'Brien, 3/6/2008
Pauline O'Hare, 2/2/2008
Jeanne Rathbone, 21/5/2008
Mary Sexton. 11/2/2008
Pat Thompson, 12/7/2004
'anonymous', 10/9/2008

NOTES TO THE TEXT

Introduction: Keeping secrets

1. Ruane, M. (2000) 'Introduction' in *The Irish Journey, Women's Stories of Abortion*, Dublin: Irish Family Planning Association.

2. Jim Mac Laughlin warns that 'new wave' emigrants from Ireland in the contemporary period are viewed by many politicians, journalists and academics as a separate category from their predecessors who were forced to emigrate through unemployment and poverty. The 'new wave', by virtue of their educational and professional qualifications, are said to voluntarily locate anywhere in the world for the purposes of enhancing their careers. Mac Laughlin, however, argues that the term 'new wave' is both misleading and misused, since the most recent surveys of Irish emigration suggest emigrants differ little by virtue of class, occupation and reasons for leaving since the 1950s. Mac Laughlin, J. (1999) 'Social Characteristics of New Wave Irish Emigration', in Mac Laughlin, J. (ed) *Location and Dislocation in Contemporary Irish Society: Emigration and Irish Identities*, Cork: Cork University Press.

3. Mahon, E., Conlon, C., & Dillon, L. (1998) *Women and Crisis Pregnancy*, Dublin: The Stationery Office.

4. Lennon, M., McAdam, M. and O'Brien, J. (1988) *Across the Water: Irish Women's Lives in Britain*, London: Virago Press.

5. An example is: Gray, B. (2000) 'From "Ethnicity" to "Diaspora": 1980s Emigration and "Multicultural" London' in Bielenberg, A. (ed) *The Irish Diaspora*, London: Longman.

6. Rochford, M. (2008) *Gilded Shadows*, Birmingham: Tia Publishing.

CHAPTER 1

Just another crisis pregnancy

1. A version of 'Sure we're all paddies over here' by Ann Rossiter first appeared in *Left Republican Review 5* (2003): Belfast.

2. A 'Loyalist' is seen as an ultra-Unionist, i.e. one who wishes to remain part of the Union of Great Britain and Northern Ireland, and who would defend the Union by violent means if necessary.

3. 'Paddy' is a pejorative term referring to an Irish man who is seen as stupid, drunken, violent, and incomprehensible. The English language is replete with anti-Irishisms like 'Paddy', ranging from 'throwing a paddy', 'in a bit of a paddy' to 'paddywaggon' (police van).

4. 'Plastic Paddy' is said to have been invented in the 1980s and is often used abusively (even by the Irish themselves) to describe second and third-generation Irish people born in Britain, but who are not seen as the 'genuine article', i.e. Irish born. Brian Dooley (2004) *Choosing the Green?: Second Generation Irish and the Cause of Ireland*, Belfast: Beyond the Pale, explores the subject in depth.

5. The origins of 'Orange' lie in the Dutch House of Orange. Its origins in Ulster lie in the defeat of the English Catholic King James at the Battle of the Boyne in 1690 by the Protestant King William of Orange (King Billy), who ascended the English, Scots and Irish thrones to rule jointly with his wife Mary. Taking its name from that event in history is the Orange Order, a militantly sectarian and exclusively Protestant organisation formed in 1795, one which has been closely linked in modern times to the two Unionist parties. Traditionally, the Orange Order's marching season beginning on the 12th July each year is a form of popular expression of Unionism. The marching symbolically claims the entire territory of Northern Ireland, to be defended at all costs from republican and nationalist advances.

6. Catholic (not necessarily practising), republican, and nationalist are terms used to refer to the minority population in Northern Ireland. 'Nationalist' signifies a person committed to achieving a united Ireland, whereas 'republican' has a more radical connotation implying willingness to engage in armed combat for the same ends.

7. 'Blighty' comes from the Hindi *bilayati* (foreign). It is used as term for 'Britain' and came into common usage in the First World

War when a popular song, 'Take me back to dear old Blighty, put me on the train for London town', was sung by British soldiers in France.

8. Last updated on 25 October 2008, the figures for the Republic add up to 150,000 plus abortions since 1968, rising steadily from 64 abortions in 1968 to over 6,000 per year between 1999 and 2004. Since reaching its peak at 6,673 in 2001 numbers have been declining and stand at 4,686 in 2007.

For the North the figures from 1969 to 2007 add up to 53,000 plus; starting with 100 in 1969, surpassing 1,000 in 1973 and rising steadily to a peak of 1855 in 1990. The average since 1973 is 1,500. The figure for 2007 is 1,343.

These figures relate only to women having abortions in England and Wales providing an address in the Republic or Northern Ireland. They take no account of abortion seekers giving false British addresses. Neither do they account for an increasing number travelling to Belgium and Holland for the procedure due to the availability of cheap flights and cheaper termination fees, although this may change due to the slide of the pound against the Euro.

www.johnstonsarchive.net/policy/abortion/ab-ireland.html for the Republic

www.johnstonsarchive.net/policy/abortion/ab-uknorthireland.html for Northern Ireland.

9. Buckley, M. (1997) 'Sitting on Your Politics: The Irish Among the British and the Women Among the Irish' in Mac Laughlin, J. (ed) *Location and Dislocation in Contemporary Irish Society: Emigration and Irish Identities*, Cork: Cork University Press.

10. In 'Great hatred, little room' authored by the Irish Abortion Solidarity Campaign in the *Irish Post*, (16/1/1999).

11. Tom Hesketh (1990) entitles his book on the Irish abortion wars of the 1980s, *The Second Partitioning of Ireland: The Abortion Referendum of 1983*, Dunlaoghaire: Brandsma Books.

CHAPTER 2

Putting Irish things sexual into context

1. Augustine, The City of God (X1V, 24), cited in Ranke-Heinemann, U. (1991) Eunuchs for the Kingdom of Heaven: The Catholic Church and Sexuality, London: Penguin.

2. Ranke-Heinemann, U. (1991), ibid. p.9.

3. Levine, J. (1982) *Sisters: The Personal Story of an Irish Feminist*, Dublin: Ward River Press, p.97.

4. Brody, H. (1973) *Inishkillane, Change and Decline in the West of Ireland*, London: Faber & Faber, pp.11-112.

5. Cormac O'Grada's (1995) *Ireland: A New Economic History 1780-1939*, Oxford: Clarendon Press, is a useful source of information on a wide range of subjects including fertility, population change, land tenure, and the economic aftermath of the famine. On the role of religion, the American historian, Emmet Larkin, provides some valuable insights in his two volumes, *The Roman Catholic Church and the Creation of the Modern Irish State, 1878-1886*, Philadelphia: The American Philosophical Society, published in 1975, and *The Making of the Roman Catholic Church in Ireland, 1850-1860*, Chapel Hill: The University of North Carolina Press, published in 1980. Eugene Hynes (Spring 1978) 'The Great Hunger and Irish Catholicism', in *Societas* 8, 2, is useful, as are Joseph Lee (1978) 'Women and the Church since the Famine' in Mac Curtain and O'Corrain (eds) *Women in Irish Society, the Historical Dimension*, Dublin: Arlen House, The Women's Press, and Tom Inglis (1987) *Moral Monopoly – The Rise and Fall of the Catholic Church in Modern Ireland*, Dublin: University College Press. On the question of abortion politics and national identity, Lisa Smyth's (2005) *Abortion and Nation: The Politics of Reproduction in Contemporary Ireland*, Aldershot: Ashgate, provides a sociological interpretation. It also has a good bibliography. All of the essays in *The Abortion Papers* (1992) edited by Ailbhe Smyth and published by Attic Press, Dublin are useful background material. Myrtle Hill's (2003) *Women in Ireland: a Century of Change*, Belfast: Blackstaff Press is an historical overview of women in the two states with an unusual, and helpful, emphasis on Northern Irish women.

6. Delaney, S. (2005 – first published in 1958) *A Taste of Honey*, London: Methuen Drama.

7. O'Brien, E. (1960) *The Country Girls*, London: Hutchinson.

8. O'Brien, E. (1964) *The Girl With Green Eyes*, London: Penguin Books.

9. Durcan, P. (1985) *The Berlin Wall Café*, Belfast: Blackstaff Press.

10. McCarthy, P. (1994) *Abortion*, in Donovan, K., Norman Jeffares, A., Bennelly, B. (eds) *Ireland's Women: Writings Past and Present*, London: Kyle Cathie.

11. Enright, A. (2002) *What Are You Like?* London: Jonathan Cape.

12. Binchy, M. (1978) 'Shepherd's Bush' in Victoria Line, *Central Line: Stories of Big City Life,* London: Random House.

13. O'Connor, J. (1992) *Cowboys and Indians,* London: Flamingo.

14. Doyle, R. (1988) *The Commitments,* London: Heinemann.

15. Morrow, D. (1997) 'Suffering for Righteousness Sake? Fundamentalist Protestantism and Ulster Politics' in Shirlow, P. & McGovern, M. (eds) *Who are "the People"?* *Unionism, Protestantism and Loyalism in Northern Ireland,* London: Pluto.

16. Ranke-Heinemann, U., (1991) op. cit. p.80.

17. Augustine, *Enchiridion,* 13, 41, cited in Ranke-Heinemann, U., op. cit., pp.77-78.

18. Ranke-Heinemann, U., (1991) op. cit. pp. 77, 308.

19. Noonan Jr., J.T. (1966) *Contraception: A History of its Treatment by the Catholic Theologians and Canonists,* Harvard: Harvard University Press, p.495.

20. 'Birth Control', *Encyclopaedia Britannica* (1984), p.1071.

21. Milotte, M. (1997) *Banished Babies: The secret history of Ireland's baby export business,* Dublin: New Island Books.

22. Kavanagh, R. (2005) *Mamie Cadden: Backstreet Abortionist,* Cork: Mercier Press.

23. Rose, R. (1976) *An Outline of Fertility Control, Focusing on the Element of Abortion, in the Republic of Ireland to 1976,* unpublished PhD thesis, University of Stockholm, Sweden.

24. Rose, ibid.

25. Rose, ibid. p.173.

26. McCafferty, N. (1985) A Woman to Blame: *The Kerry Babies Case,* Dublin: Attic Press.

27. Guilbride, A. (2004) 'Infanticide: the Crime of Motherhood' in Kennedy. P. (ed), *Motherhood in Ireland: Creation and Context,* Cork: Mercier Press.

28. Connor, A. (1992) 'Abortion: Myths and Realities from the Irish Folk Tradition' in Smyth, A. (ed) *The Abortion Papers, Ireland,* Dublin: Attic Press.

29. The Reverend Richard McBrien cited in an article in the New York newspaper, *The Sun*, entitled 'Pope Offers Hope for Unbaptized Babies', dated 21/4/2007.

CHAPTER 3

'We were our bit of the Irish community': the making of the *alternative* Irish community in London.

1. Bronwen Walter (1997) 'Contemporary Irish Settlement in London: Women's Worlds, Men's Worlds' in Mac Laughlin, J. (ed) *Location and Dislocation in Contemporary Irish Society: Emigration and Irish Identities*, Cork: Cork University Press, pp. 61-93, refers to the greater number of women than men recorded in each Census as a distinctive feature of Irish settlement in London between 1861 and 1961.

2. Kennedy, R.E. (1973) *Emigration, Marriage and Fertility*, Berkeley: University of California Press.

3. Amongst others besides Kennedy who highlighted the extent of Irish women's migration and its characteristics were: Hasia Diner (1983) in *Erin's Daughters in America: Irish Immigrant Women in the Nineteenth Century*, Baltimore: John Hopkins University Press; Bronwen Walter (1991) in 'Gender and recent Irish migration to Britain', Russell King, R. (ed) *Contemporary Irish Migration*, Geographical Society of Ireland, Special Publication No.6, Dublin: 1991; Donald Harman Akenson (1993) in *The Irish Diaspora: a primer*, Belfast: The Institute of Irish Studies, and Pauric Travers (1995a) in '"There was nothing for me there": Irish female emigration, 1922-71' in O'Sullivan, P. (ed) *Irish Women and Migration*, London: Leicester University Press.

4. cited in O'Connor, K. (1974) *The Irish in Britain*, Dublin: Torc Books, p.98. McAlpine was a well-known British construction company

5. O'Connor, K. (1974) ibid. p.66.

6. O'Neill, J. (1969) *The Molly Maguires*, New York: Fawcett Publications.

7. Enoch Powell in his 'rivers of blood' speech in 1968 called for the repatriation of black immigrants in Britain before bloody confrontations took place between them and the English. He asserted that there was no way that these inherently different immigrants could ever assimilate with the English.

8. Amongst the twenty-three bombing incidents which occurred in the 1980s, the most serious were: the deaths of four guardsmen killed in Hyde Park in London in July 1982 during the Changing of the Guards ceremony, the bombing of the Grand Hotel in Brighton in October 1984 where the annual Conservative Party Conference was being held, and the deaths of ten Royal Marine bandsmen at the Royal Marines School of Music in Deal, Kent in November 1989. Among the one hundred and forty or so incidents recorded in the 1990s, the most serious were the explosion at the Baltic Exchange in the City of London in April 1992 resulting in three casualties and an estimated £800 million worth of damage, the Bishopsgate lorry bomb in April 1993 in which one person was killed and the ensuing damage estimated at £600 million, the Canary Wharf bomb in February 1996, killing one person and causing an estimated £100 million worth of damage, and the explosion near the Arndale Shopping Centre in Manchester in June 1996 which resulted in damage worth £400 million. Cited in McGladdery, G. (2006), *The Provisional IRA in England. The Bombing Campaign 1973-1997*, Dublin: Irish Academic Press.

9. Hillyard, P. (1993) *Suspect Community, People's Experience of the Prevention of Terrorism Acts in Britain*, London: Pluto.

10. Sean Hutton of the Federation of Irish Societies (FIS) points out that Liverpool-based Tommy Walsh, who was a national officer of the Federation in the 1970s, was highly active in his opposition to the PTA. In this context he also mentions Fr. Joe Taffe, a priest working at the Irish Welfare and Advice Centre in Birmingham, affiliated to FIS. Hutton says of Taffe, that although 'deeply suspicious of communism and, I would say, highly conservative [presumably on sexuality and reproductive rights] was also absolutely fearless on issues like the PTA.' (personal communication with author dated 4/7/2008).

11. Herbert, M. (2001) *The wearing of the green: a political history of the Irish in Manchester*, Manchester: Irish in Britain Representation Group, p.177.

12. The Limerick Association, for instance, has had such a clause in its constitution. However, this was amended in February 2007 to read 'The Limerick Association is a non-party political and non-sectarian organisation.' Email correspondence between author and Patrick Cullinane, 4/9/2008.

13. Coughlan, A. (1994) 'C. Desmond Greaves – Politician and Historian', in O'Ceallaigh, D. (ed) *Reconsiderations of Irish*

History and Culture, Dublin: Leirmheas. Herbert, M. (2001) op. cit., pp.135-139. O'Connor, K. (1974) op. cit. p.50.

14. Troops Out was set up in September 1973 by students, trade unionists and ex-soldiers. The organisation's founding principal was 'Self-determination for the Irish People' and 'Withdrawal of British troops from Northern Ireland'. Its magazine *Troops Out* began publishing in October 1977. Herbert, M. (2001), op. cit. p.162.

The first of the Women and Ireland groups was set up in London in 1972 to discuss and publicise the war in Ireland and to highlight the crucial role being played by women, especially in the nationalist and republican communities. By the early 1980s, a network of Women and Ireland groups existed in twelve British cities from Bristol to Dundee. Rossiter, A. (1991) 'Bringing the margins into the centre: a review of aspects of Irish women's emigration' in Hutton. S. & Stewart, P. (eds) *Ireland's Histories: Aspects of State, Society and Ideology*, London: Routledge.

The Armagh Group, formed in 1980 to work specifically on republican women prisoners, especially those being held in Armagh Jail, Northern Ireland, is discussed in Rossiter, A. (2005) '*Not our cup of tea', Nation, Empire and the Irish Question in English Feminism in the 1970s and 1980s*, unpublished PhD thesis, London South Bank University.

The Irish in Britain Representation Group (IBRG) was formed in 1981 with a civil rights and social justice agenda directed against the actions of the British government and army in Northern Ireland and the treatment of the Irish community in Britain.

The Labour Committee on Ireland was established in 1980 and had a radical agenda to raise the Irish Question within the Labour Party and trade union movement, and to push for a political rather than a military solution to 'the Troubles'. Herbert, M. (2001) op. cit. pp. 177-179; 182-186.

The Wolfe Tone Society is a republican support group which has worked in London for the past quarter of a century.

15. O'Briain, M. (1981) *Irish Migrants in London: Motivation and Social Orientation*, unpublished M.Phil thesis, City University, London, p.169.

16. O'Connor, K. (1974) op. cit. p.145.

17. *Irish Times*, 25/3/1948 cited in Travers, P. (1995b) 'Emigration and Gender: The Case of Ireland, 1922-60' in O'Dowd, M. &

195

Wichert, S. (eds) *Chattel, Servant or Citizen: Women's Status in Church, State and Society*, Belfast: Institute of Irish Studies, p.190.

18. Sharkey, S. (1993) 'Frontier Issues: Irish Women's Texts and Contexts', *Women: A Cultural Review* 4.

19. O'Clubhan, C. (1986) 'Sexuality for Export' in Dublin Lesbian and Gay Collectives (eds) *Out For Ourselves: The Lives of Irish Lesbians and Gay Men*, Dublin: Dublin Lesbian and Gay Collectives and Women's Community Press, p.88.

20. Smyth, C. (1995) 'Keeping it Close: Emigration in England' in O'Carroll, I. and Collins, E. (eds) *Lesbian and Gay Visions of Ireland: Towards the Twenty-first Century*, London: Cassell, pp. 221-232.

21. O'Clubhan, C. (1986) op. cit. pp. 87-88.

22. O'Carroll, I. (1995) 'Editors' Introduction' in O'Carroll, I. and Collins, E. (eds), op. cit. pp. 2-3.

23. O'Briain, M. (1981), op. cit. pp.122-123.

24. Quoted in O'Connor, K. (1974), op. cit. p.60.

25. O'Briain, M. (1981), op. cit. p.123, citing a Camden Irish Centre publication (1977): *Helping Hands: Outlines of the Origin and Development of the Irish Centre – over 21 years*.

26. Higgins, A. (1988) 'Manchester Childhood, 1930s: A strong feeling of roots', in Lennon, M., McAdam, M., O'Brien, J. (eds) *Across the Water: Irish Women's Lives in Britain*, London: Virago, p.150.

27. Hickman, M. (1995) *Religion, Class and Identity*, Hampshire: Avebury.

28. Gilley, S. (1988) 'Catholics and their Church in Britain, c.1880-1939', *Warwick Working Papers in Social History*, University of Warwick.

29. Connolly, G. (1985) 'Irish and Catholic: Myth or Reality? Another sort of Irish and the renewal of the clerical profession among Catholics in England, 1791-1918' in Swift, R. and Gilley, S. (eds) *The Irish in the Victorian City*, Beckenham: Croom Helm.

30. Kells, M. (1995) '"I'm myself and nobody else': gender and ethnicity among young middle-class Irish women in London", in O'Sullivan, P. (1995), op. cit.

31. Interview with Joan Neary, 2/10/2007. Hereafter, all references to Joan relate to this interview.

32. Interview with Joanne O'Brien, 3/6/2008. Hereafter, all references to Joanne relate to this interview.

33. Marian Larragy, email correspondence with author, 5/1/2009. All references to Marian hereafter refer to this email unless otherwise stated.

34. Interview with Jeanne Rathbone 21/5/2008. Hereafter, all references to Jeanne relate to this interview.

35. Shere Hite is an American-born German sex educator and feminist. Amongst the many works she has published is *The Hite Report on the Family: Growing Up Under Patriarchy* (1994).

36. Charlotte Despard (1844-1939), a British-born, later Irish-based suffragist, novelist and Sinn Fein activist. Despard joined Hanna Sheehy-Skeffington and Margaret Cousins to form the Irish Women's Franchise League. During the Irish War of Independence, together with Maud Gonne, she formed the Women's Prisoners' Defence League in support of republican prisoners. Two biographies have been published, one by Andro Linklater (1980) *An Unhusbanded Life: Charlotte Despard, Suffragette, Socialist and Sinn Feiner*, London: Hutchinson. The second is by Margaret Mulvihill (1989) *Charlotte Despard: A biography*, London: Pandora.

37. Interview with 'anonymous' on 10/9/2008.

38. Brid Boland, written communication with author, 12/8/2008.

39. London Irish Women's Centre, *Irish Women, Our Lives – Our Identity*, Report of 1987 Irish Women's Conference.

40. Two days after the London bombings of July 7, 2005, Tony Blair, Britain's prime minister, sourced 'the problem', or as he saw it, the existential threat to the British way of life, as residing in large measure in the heartland of British Islam. At one stroke, the policy of multiculturalism was erased to be replaced by a process of assimilation of all ethnic minorities, but particularly of Muslims.

41. Lester, A. (1967) *Essays and Speeches by Roy Jenkins*, London: Collins, p.267.

42. Gray, B. (2000) 'From "Ethnicity to "Diaspora": 1980s Emigration and "Multicultural" London' in Bielenberg, A. (ed) *The Irish Diaspora*, London: Pearson, p.71

43. Ali, Y. (1992) 'Muslim Women and the Politics of Ethnicity and Culture in Northern England' in Sahgal, G. and Yuval-Davis, N.

(eds) *Refusing Holy Orders: Women and Fundamentalism in Britain*, London: Virago, p.104.

44. Kundnani, A. (2007) *The End of Tolerance: Racism in 21st Century Britain*, London: Pluto, p. 47.

45. Patel, P. (2003) 'Shifting terrains: old struggles for new?' in Gupta, R., *From Homebreakers to Jailbreakers: Southall Black Sisters*, London: Zed.

46. Southall Black Sisters (1990) *Against the Grain: A Celebration of Survival and Struggle*, London: SBS.

47. Interview with 'anonymous', 10/9/08.

CHAPTER 4

Beginnings and Bloodlines: The first phase of the Irish Women's Abortion Support Group (IWASG)

1. A true story by Ann Rossiter.

2. This is a reference to the Required Standard Operating Principles introduced by the Department of Health in 2001.

3. Interview with Ellen Mullin, 24/10/2008. Hereafter, all references to Ellen relate to this interview.

4. Rose, R. (1976) *An Outline of Fertility Control, Focusing on the Element of Abortion, in the Republic of Ireland to 1976*, unpublished PhD, University of Stockholm, Sweden, p.31.

5. Finnegan, F. (2001) *Do Penance or Perish: Magdalen Asylums in Ireland*, Oxford: Oxford University Press, pp. ix, 242.

6. O'Faolain, N. (1996) *Are You Somebody?* Dublin: New Island.

7. Irish Women's Abortion Support Group (1988) 'Across the Water', *Feminist Review* No.29, Spring, pp. 68-69.

8. Escort, a support group based in Liverpool, operated with financial help from the National Union of Students. Escort's predecessor was Liverpool Abortion Services (LASS) which gave evidence to the International Tribunal on Abortion in Northern Ireland in 1987. A profile of Escort is given in Melissa Thompson's documentary, *Like a Ship in the Night* on DVD, 2002: www.likeashipinthenight.com

9. Quoted in Fisher, K. (1998) 'Women's Experience of Abortion before the 1967 Abortion Act: a Study of South Wales c.1930-1950' in Lee, E. (ed) *Abortion Law and Politics Today*, Houndmills: Macmillan, p.29.

10. Simms, M. (1998) 'Abortion Law Reform in Britain in the 1960s – What were the Issues Then?' in Lee, E. (ed), ibid. pp. 5-10.

11. Paintin, D. (1988) 'A Medical View of Abortion in the 1960s' in Lee, E. (ed), ibid. pp. 12-18.

12. McCarthy, A. (2004) 'Oh Mother Where Art Thou?': Irish Mothers and Irish Fiction in the Twentieth Century' in Kennedy, P. (ed) *Motherhood in Ireland*, Cork: Mercier Press.

13. Myrtle Hill (2003) says that in 1926 14.5% of married women in Northern Ireland worked, as opposed to 5.6% in the southern state, op. cit. p.100.

14. Nic Ghiolla Phadraig, M., Clancy, P. (1995) 'Marital Fertility and Family Planning in Dublin' in Colgan, I. (ed) *Irish Family Studies, Selected Papers*, Dublin: Family Studies Centre, University College Dublin.

15. Eurostat (2000) *Statistics in Focus*, Luxembourg: Office of Official Publications of the European Community, No.5.

16. Conroy, P. (2004) 'Maternity Confined – the Struggle for Fertility Control' in Kennedy, P. (ed) op. cit. p.129.

17. Courtney, D. (1995) 'Demographic Structure and Change in the Republic of Ireland and Northern Ireland' in Clancy, P., Drudy, S., Lynch, K., O'Dowd, L. (eds) *Irish Society: Sociological Perspectives*, Dublin: Institute of Public Administration.

CHAPTER 5

The work of the Irish Women's Abortion Support Group (IWASG)

1. Riddick, R. (1992) 'Towards a Feminist Morality of Choice' in Smyth, A. (ed) *The Abortion Papers Ireland*, Dublin: Attic Press, pp.191-192.

2. Figures quoted in 'Spanish Women and the Alton Bill' by the Spanish Women's Abortion Support Group (SWASG), (1988) *Feminist Review* No. 29, Spring, p.73.

3. Interview with Iris Lyle, 27/10/2007. Hereafter, all references to Iris relate to this interview.

4. Interview with Isabel Ros Lopez, 20/11/2007. Hereafter, all references to Isabel Ros relate to this interview.

5. Interview with Kate Duke, 10/1/2008. Hereafter, all references to Kate relate to this interview.

6. Irish Women's Abortion Support Group (1988) 'Across the Water', *Feminist Review* No. 29, Spring, p.70.

7. Interview with Noreen Byrne, 29/10/2007. Hereafter, all references to Noreen relate to this interview unless stated otherwise.

8. Interview with Blanca Fernandez, 21/2/2008. Hereafter, all references to Blanca relate to this interview.

9. Interview with Pat Thompson, 12/7/2004. Hereafter, all references to Pat relate to this interview.

10. Interview with Ann Hayes, 12/11/2007. Hereafter, all references to Ann relate to this interview.

11. Interview with Gautam Appa, 10/3/2008.

12. Agenda: *Information Day. Irish Women's Abortion Support Group, Saturday 7th December 1985*, IWASG papers, listing: 1) Legal Aspects and Information, 2) Medical Information, 3) PAS Procedure, 4) Emotional Aspects/Support.

13. *Report on Press Conference with Noreen Byrne, Director of the Well Woman Centre, Dublin, on 31/1/83 at 4pm in the Library, Conway Hall, Red Lion Square, W1, hosted by the Irish Women's Abortion Support Group*, IWASG papers.

14. Posters and leaflets, IWASG papers.

15. Posters and leaflets, IWASG papers.

16. Sponsorship form, IWASG papers.

17. IWASG Minutes of meeting, 1/6/1986, IWASG papers.

18. Interview with Catherine Boyle, 12/1/2008. Hereafter, all references to Catherine relate to this interview.

19. Gray, B. (2003) 'From "Ethnicity" to "Diaspora": 1980s Emigration and "Multicultural" London in Bielenberg, A. *The Irish Diaspora*, Harlow: Pearson Education, p.73.

20. Marian Larragy, email communication, 6/1/2009. Hereafter, all references to Marian refer to this email.

21. Interview with Angie Birtill, 28/1/2008. Hereafter, all references to Angie relate to this interview.

22. Brid Boland, written communication with author, August 2008. Hereafter, all references to Brid relate to this communication.

23. The 6th London Irish Women's Centre Conference was on the subject of mental health: *Irish Women and Mental Health: Culture & Context, Conference Report*, October 1998: London Irish Women's Centre.

Roots & Realities, A Profile of Irish Women in London 1993 was published by the London Irish Women's Centre in 1993.

24. Interview with Brian McCarthy, 3/2/2008. Hereafter, all references to Brian relate to this interview.

25. Buckley, M. (1997) 'Sitting on Your Politics: The Irish Among the British and the Women Among the Irish' in Mac Laughlin, J. (ed) *Location and Dislocation in Contemporary Irish Society: Emigration and Irish Identities*, Cork: Cork University Press, p.125

26. Mahon, E., Conlon, C., and Dillon, L. (1998) *Women and Crisis Pregnancy: A Report Presented to the Department of Health and Children*, Dublin: The Stationery Office, p.45.

CHAPTER 6

The Irish abortion seeker as a 'special case'

1. Buckley, M. (1997) 'Sitting on Your Politics: The Irish Among the British and the Women Among the Irish' in Mac Laughlin, J. (ed) *Location and Dislocation in Contemporary Irish Society: Emigration and Irish Identities*, Cork: Cork University Press, p.125.

2. Interview with Mary Sexton 11/2/2008. Hereafter, all references to Mary relate to this interview unless otherwise stated.

3. O'Hare, P. (1970) 'Abortion seeking women from Ireland – What are their counselling needs?' in Lee, E. and Lattimer, M. (eds) *Issues in Pregnancy Counselling: What Do Women Need and Want?* London: Pro-Choice Forum, p.58.

4. ibid. p.60.

5. ibid. p.60.

6. ibid. p.60

7. Hadley, J. (1996) Abortion: Between Freedom and Necessity, London: Virago, p xi.

8. Duran, M.A. and Gallego, M.T. (1986) 'The women's movement in Spain and the new Spanish democracy' in Dahlerup, D. (ed) *The New Women's Movement: Feminism and Political Power in Europe and the USA*, London: Sage.

9. Coogan, T.P. (1993) *De Valera, Long Fellow, Long Shadow*, London: Hutchinson, p.475.

10. Smith, D. M. (1969) *Italy: A Modern History*, Ann Arbor: The University of Michigan Press, pp.8, 14-16, 39-41.

11. McCarthy, D. (1987) *The Dawning of Democracy: Ireland 1800-1870*, Dublin: Helicon, pp. 110-111.

12. Larkin, E. (1980) *The Making of the Roman Catholic Church in Ireland, 1850-1860*, Chapel Hill: The University of North Carolina Press.

13. Morrow, D. (1997) 'Suffering for Righteousness Sake? Fundamentalist Protestantism and Ulster Politics' in Shirlow, P. & McGovern, M. (eds.) *Who are "the People"?, Unionism, Protestantism and Loyalism in Northern Ireland*, London: Pluto, p.56.

14. McVeigh, R. (2002) 'Nick, Nack, Paddywhack: Anti-Irish racism and the racialisation of Irishness', in Lentin, R. and McVeigh, R., *Racism and Anti-Racism in Ireland*, Belfast: Beyond the Pale, p.136.

15. Robinson, M. (1992) Speech given to Waterford women's groups quoted in *Irish Times*, 20 February.

16. Monsivais, C. (2000) Paper read at the presentation of the book, *Las Mil y Una...(la herida de Paulina)* by Elena Poniatowska, Mexico City: Plaza Janes, cited in Lamas, M., and Bissell, S. (2000) 'Abortion and Politics in Mexico: Context is All' in *Reproductive Health Matters*, Vol.8, No.16, pp.10-23.

17. Irish Women's Abortion Support Group (1988) 'Across the Water' *Feminist Review* No. 29, Spring, p.68.

18. McVeigh, R. (2002) op. cit. p.137.

19. Interview with Annie Campbell, 8/10/2004. Hereafter, all references to Annie relate to this interview.

CHAPTER 7

Introducing IWASG Women

1. De Burgh, S. (2000) 'Preface' to *The Irish Journey, Women's Stories of Abortion*, Dublin: Irish Family Planning Association, p.4.

2. Cited in Levine, J. (1982) Sisters: The Personal Story of an Irish Feminist, Dublin: Ward River Press, pp. 94-111.

3. Hug, C. (1999) *The Politics of Sexual Morality in Ireland*, London: Macmillan, p.168.

4. Tatalovich, R. & Daynes, B.W. (1981) *The Politics of Abortion: A Study of Community Conflict in Public Policy Making*, New York: Praeger, p.12.

5. Levine, J. (1982) op. cit. p.95.

6. Levine, J. (1982) op. cit. pp. 174-182.

7. Bassnett, S. (1986) *Feminist Experiences: The Women's Movement in Four Cultures*, London: Allen & Unwin, pp. 94, 95.

8. Connolly, L. (2003) *The Irish Women's Movement: From Revolution to Devolution*, Dublin: The Lilliput Press, pp. 132-3.

9. Interview with Joanne O'Brien, 3/6/2008. Hereafter, all references to Joanne relate to this interview.

10. Interview with Pauline O'Hare, 2/2/2008. Hereafter, all references to Pauline relate to this interview.

11. Interview with Teresa Dunne, 2/1/2008. All references to Teresa relate to this interview.

12. Interview with Catherine Boyle, 12/1/2008. All references to Catherine relate to this interview.

13. Interview with Annie Campbell, 8/10/04. All references to Annie relate to this interview.

14. Delmar, R. (1986) 'What is Feminism?' in Mitchell, J. & Oakley, A. (eds) *What is Feminism?* Oxford: Basil Blackwell.

15. see The Northern Ireland Abortion Law Reform Association (1989) *Abortion in Northern Ireland: The Report of an International Tribunal*: Belfast: Beyond the Pale, pp. 42, 43.

16. *Green Paper on Abortion* (c.1999, no date given), Dublin: The Stationery Office.

17. Mahon, E., Conlon, C. & Dillon, L. (1998) *Women and Crisis Pregnancy*, Dublin: The Stationery Office.

CHAPTER 8

The Irish Abortion Solidarity Campaign (Iasc)

1. Goretti Horgan, interview, 5/1/2009.

2. Voice for Choice: http://www.vfc.org.uk/about/

3. Letter from Diane Abbott MP to Alliance for Choice, 22/10/2008.

4. http://edmi.parliament.uk/EDMi/EDMDetails.aspx?EDMID=37671&SESSION=899

5. 'Women wage campaign against the growth of fundamentalism', *The Independent*, London, 16/5/1990.

6. On 18th June 1992 a majority of citizens of the Republic voted in favour of ratifying the Maastricht Treaty which supplemented and modified the European Community Treaties already in existence. It includes Protocol 17, inserted by the government of the Republic, which provides that, 'Nothing in the Treaty on European Union, or in the Treaties establishing the European Communities, or in the Treaties or Acts modifying or supplementing those Treaties, shall affect the application in Ireland of Article 40.3.3 of the Constitution of Ireland [which grants equal civil rights to foetus and mother].'

7. Iasc, 'Great hatred, little room', London: *Irish Post*, 16/1/1999.

8. Cited in Gomperts, R. (2002) *Women on Waves*, Amsterdam: Women on Waves, p.2.

9. Ferry, J., 'The abortion ship's doctor', *The Guardian*, 14/11/2007.

10. Gomperts, R. (2002) *Women on Waves*, Amsterdam: Women on Waves, pp. 31-33.

11. ibid. pp. 69, 71.

12. Information on the latest activities of Women on Waves can be had at: www.womenonwaves.org

The new government of the Portuguese Socialist Party conducted a referendum in April 2007, as a result of which President Cavaco Silva ratified a law allowing women to obtain abortions until the 10th week of pregnancy.

13. Goretti Horgan, Interview, 27/11/2008.

14. Quoted in the Manifesto of the Northern Ireland Women's Coalition, 1996, cited in Fearon, K. (1999) *Women's Work: The Story of the Northern Ireland Women's Coalition*, Belfast: Blackstaff Press, p.138.

15. Bruce, S. (1992) *The Red Hand: Protestant Paramilitaries in Northern Ireland*, Oxford: Oxford University Press.

16. Cited in Kelley, K. (1982) *The Longest War: Northern Ireland and the IRA*, London: Zed Books, p.146.

17. *Taigh* is a pejorative term for Catholic nationalist or republican.

18. Anderson, D. (1994) *14 May Days: The Inside Story of the Loyalist Strike of 1974*, Dublin: Gill and Macmillan.

19. David Ervine, quoted in *Women's News*, Belfast, November 2001.

20. Keane, M. P. (2003) 'Exploring Difference – Women's Cross-Border/Cross-Community Cultural Exchange and Activism' in *Women's Studies Review*, Vol. 9, Galway: National University of Ireland, pp.161-174.

21. Hill, M. (2003a) 'Lessons and Legacies: Feminist Activism in the North c1970-2000' in *Women's Studies Review*, ibid. p. 145.

22. Thompson, M. (2007) *Like a Ship in the Night*, DVD www.likeashipinthenight.com

23. See, for example, Hill, M. (2003a) ibid. pp.135-150

24. A detailed analysis by Mary Paul Keane, op. cit., who has worked in the field and researched for a doctorate on the subject of women's community groups, highlights one element amongst several of this new phenomenon, namely the European Union's Special Support Programme for Peace and Reconciliation in the period 1995-1999. Keane says that under Round 1 of the Peace Programme 40 million Euros was exclusively allocated to cross-border community reconciliation and to business and cultural contacts in the six border counties of the Republic and of Northern Ireland, a substantial part of which went to women's organisations. To this end about 25 women's development workers were employed in the Northern Irish border counties resulting in grass-roots women's groups generating a membership of almost 12,500. In the Southern border region she states that there were about 140 women-based projects, each with a membership of between 50 and 300. Much of the work of these groups involved making cross-border contacts, acknowledging the trauma of 'the Troubles', dealing with the injury and suffering caused, embracing healing processes, pursuing community education and cross-cultural programmes.

25. Hill, M. (2003b) *Women in Ireland, A Century of Change*, Belfast: The Blackstaff Press, pp. 226-227.

26. Ward, E. & O'Donovan, O. (1996) 'Networks of Women's Groups and Politics in Ireland: What (Some) Women Think, in *UCG Women's Studies Centre Review*, Vol.4, Galway: Women's Studies Centre p. 17.

27. Letter sent by Alliance for Choice to all Westminster MPs on 8/7/2008.

28. Kiss, Y. (1991) 'The Second "No": Women in Hungary', *Feminist Review*, No.19, 1991.

29. Watson, P. (1996) The Rise of Masculinism in Eastern Europe' in Threlfall, M. (ed) *Mapping the Women's Movement*, London: Verso, p.221.

30. Budgeon, S. (2001) 'Emergent Feminist (?) Identities: Young Women and the Practice of Micropolitics', *The European Journal of Women's Studies*, 8:1, p.25.

APPENDIX

23rd September, 2001

The Other Irish Journey

A survey update of Northern Irish women attending
British abortion clinics, 2000/2001

Ann Rossiter and Mary Sexton

Executive summary

Research objectives

The survey update of Northern Irish (NI) women attending British abortion clinics had five aims:

1. To update Helen Axby's 1994 survey for Marie Stopes International (MSI);
2. To seek additional relevant information;
3. To contextualise the findings by interviewing NI women, and also non-NI women, based in Britain, requesting abortions at the same clinics;
4. To contrast NI and non-NI abortion-seekers' experiences in a number of key areas;
5. To highlight the difficulties involved in NI abortion seekers' journeys to Britain.

To achieve these aims, four categories of information were solicited from respondents. Firstly, a personal profile. Secondly, details of the consultation and the referral process. Thirdly, the attitudes of individuals concerned, their partners, families and friends, as well as those of professionals, such As GPs. Finally, particular emphasis was placed on ascertaining the difficulties travel to Britain presented.

Key findings, quantitative and qualitative

(Findings, both quantitative and qualitative, refer to NI women unless otherwise stated).

- 95% support the extension to Northern Ireland of the British 1967 Abortion Act under which they accessed their abortion in Britain.

- 95% would have preferred to have their abortions in Northern Ireland.

- While awaiting progressive legislative change in Northern Ireland, most NI interviewees expressed the wish to have their abortions in Britain funded by the National Health Service (NHS).

- Some non-NI women reported difficulties in obtaining an NHS-funded abortion.

- There was widespread mistrust of GPs. Just over one in four (27%) NI women consulted GPs about their abortion choice. Some non-NI women also reported an unwillingness to approach their own GP.

- Those who did consult their GP were often dissatisfied. Some women felt they qualified for an abortion in Northern Ireland, but found their GP confused about their rights under the law.

- Abortion is accessed across a wide age spectrum in Northern Ireland, from teenagers to women aged 40+ (52% were under 25 and 48% between the ages of 25 to 40+).

- Those in employment accounted for 63%; those in education for 24%; those unemployed (including full-time home workers) accounted for 13%.

- A wide range of sources were tapped for information, including fpaNI (29%), the Yellow Pages (27%), friends and relatives (15%), the internet (5%), and women's centres (1%).

- More than half (55%) discussed their abortion decision with others, primarily their partners, friends and families, belying the 'secrecy tag' applied to Irish women. Non-NI women displayed similar patterns.

- Two out of three (68%) NI women said they knew of others' abortions.

- 61% of NI women referred themselves to the clinic.

- Almost half (44%) had to borrow money. Non-NI women who financed their own abortions also had to borrow.

- Day-care abortion services for NI women are a mixed blessing. The benefits to those with work and childcare constraints do not necessarily extend to those unable to afford the high costs of day return flights. Those from rural areas needing late-night public transport are similarly disadvantaged.

Methodology

One hundred and fifty-five questionnaires were completed by NI abortion-seekers in a six-month period from October, 2000 to March, 2001. Of these, 50 were completed at the Family Planning Association (fpaNI) in Belfast following clients' consultation and prior to the journey to clinics in Britain. The residue (105) was completed at MSI centres in London and Essex just prior to clients' abortions.

To supplement the quantitative research, interviews of 30 NI women who had completed questionnaires were conducted at MSI centres. The core interview was a structured one requiring an approximate 30-minute response time. However, interviewees were encouraged to comment on certain issues at length where their appointment schedule at the clinic allowed. There were only three refusals to requests for an interview. Equally, few NI women were reported by clinic staff as refusing to complete the questionnaire.

A further 30 interviews of non-NI women, resident in Britain, also took place at MSI centres. These lasted between 15 and 30 minutes, again depending on the flexibility of their schedules. The non-NI interviewees were not asked to complete the questionnaire, as this was viewed as too specific to the Northern Irish situation to have relevance for them.

While the sampling procedure cannot be described as random sampling in the strict statistical sense, the selection of NI respondents was entirely independent of interviewers. A stack of survey forms was left at the centres which staff requested clients to complete. At the MSI centres, an interview was requested of those filling in the forms. When NI clients agreed, staff contacted the interviewers. In contrast, the corresponding cohort of 30 non-NI women was selected as a result of ad hoc visits by the interviewers to the clinics.

The figure of 155 completed questionnaires was intended to match that of the 1994 survey. It was borne in mind that the sample amounted to about 10% of the yearly total of abortions officially recorded as performed on NI women at British clinics, although the real figure is probably much higher.[1] The sample of 30 in-depth interviews of non-Irish women was planned to draw out differences and similarities in the experiences of the two groups.

The questionnaire format matched that of the 1994 survey in all important respects, but was expanded to include greater detail on,

---

[1] The Office for National Statistics' (ONS) figure for 1999 was 1,430. However, the number of women giving false British addresses or the address of a relative or friend living in Britain in considered to be quite high, although evidence is anecdotal. The abortions of these women are included, not in the ONS figure for Northern Ireland, but in those for England and Wales.

among other things, accessing the abortion, the consultation and referral process, and the journey involved in reaching the clinic.

The question posed in the 1994 survey on religious background (asking: Protestant, Catholic, Other, None) was omitted because it was deemed unsuited to the growing ethnic and religious diversity of contemporary Northern Irish society.[2] Furthermore, to ascertain the impact of personal religious belief, or lack of it, on women opting for abortion, would have required an in-depth study beyond the limitations of this survey. The diverse backgrounds of non-Irish interviewees also informed this decision.

Dr. Gautam Appa of the London School of Economics provided support on the statistical analysis of the results.

Introduction

Although the emigrant journey is deeply etched in the Irish consciousness, that of the abortion seeker rarely features in migration lore. This may be due to problems of categorisation: after all, the abortion seeker is not embarking on a quest to improve her economic welfare, but neither is she bound for a holiday destination. One Irish writer has likened the phenomenon to being 'on the run' (Buckley, 1997) and another to 'Ireland's hidden Diaspora' (Ruane, 2000). More poignantly, the journey might be described as asylum-seeking, however temporary, especially if its covert nature, the fear of persecution and the loneliness associated with it are taken into account.

While the journey, and the abortion experience generally, have been explored in the media and in more depth in academic theses, these endeavours can only go some way to plumb the depths of pain and paradox inevitable when an increasing number of women choose to terminate their pregnancy, but are largely barred from doing so on their own turf. Absent from the welter of words are detailed and reflective commentaries by the abortion seekers themselves, especially by those from Northern Ireland, which could help place the experience in context and normalise it.[3]

---

[2]Ethnic minorities currently represent 2% of Northern Ireland's 1.7m population. The Chinese community numbers about 8,000, followed by people from other EU countries. There are some 3,000 people from India, Pakistan and Bangladesh, and 1,500 from various from various African countries. (*Guardian*, 12 September, 2001). Religions practised amongst minorities in Northern Ireland include Buddhism, Hinduism, Islam and Judaism.

[3]In contrast, three Southern Irish women, visually fully identified, have spoken of their abortions in England on a television programme (*50,000 Secret Journeys*, RTE, 26/3/94). One of these women who was identified visually and by name, also spoke on Northern Irish television (*The Kelly Show*, UTV, 20/1/92) and on British television (*A Woman's Fight to Choose*, Channel 4,

The opportunity to listen to the views of NI women attending British abortion clinics, and to discuss their experiences in some depth, occurred following the decision taken by MSI to update the survey conducted at their clinics by Helen Axby in 1994. While the current update has replicated the broad parameters of the 1994 survey in providing statistical evidence on a range of issues concerned with women's abortion experience, interviewees were encouraged to comment at length where possible.

Any discussion of Northern Ireland and abortion, written or verbal, immediately elicits a string of negatives: 'It's a "no go" area, just listen to the priests and the politicians going on', 'Nobody will talk about it, if you do, you'll get door-stepped', and, 'Just imagine them at school/college/work muttering "baby killer" under their breath. You would just be hounded out', and so on. The cycle of women being silenced, and in turn, silencing themselves, spins on.

The authors' experience of working on this survey could not have been more different. Nearly all the women approached were only too happy to talk about their abortion experience; in fact, they seemed relieved to be able to do so in a 'neutral and secular' space, so to speak. Their thoughtful replies to questions cast them, not in the mould of 'poor, brave, wee girls', the passive victims of church and state that academics, journalists and writers are wont to portray, but of women strong in their resolve to exercise their right of choice. They faced the same dilemmas as women everywhere seeking an abortion. Added to this, they had the burden of negotiating a path between the choice they had made and the dominant public view of abortion in Northern Ireland.

What is clearly evident from the survey and interviews is that the complex of issues, and above all, the practicalities faced by NI abortion-seekers, requires careful deconstruction to avoid stereotyping.

Most striking was the determination of women with unwanted pregnancies to overcome insurmountable obstacles to have an abortion. They came from different class, educational backgrounds, from across a wide age spectrum, and seemingly, from both the major communities in Northern Ireland. Some were lone parents; some were married or in relationships and had children. Many

---

15/11/97). Amongst others, June Levine, (1982), a Dublin journalist, has written of her abortion experience. More recently, a collection of abortion stories, but by unidentified women, was published by the Irish Family Planning Association (Ruane, ed., Dublin, 2000)

displayed anger at the ordeal involved in accessing their abortion, as well as at their lack of rights as British citizens. It was also instructive to learn that young – and often, not so young – NI women frequently indicated an acceptance of abortion as a fact of life, albeit a fraught one.

The reality of abortion in Northern Ireland

Despite attempts by politicians, religious leaders and the organised, anti-choice lobby to obfuscate it, abortion as a reality in the Northern Irish experience is already well established with the publication of statistics and data by the Office for National Statistics (ONS) at regular intervals. These 'reality checks' confirm that currently almost 1,500 women divulging Northern Ireland addresses attending abortion clinics annually in England and Wales are availing of the provisions of the British 1967 Abortion Act. It is estimated that at least 40,000 women have travelled from Northern Ireland in the last 20 years to pay for a private abortion (fpaNI, 2001).

Over a number of years, the reality of abortion has been highlighted by the work of a number of tribunals, commissions and surveys. For instance, there were the findings of the 1987 International Tribunal which were later published (NIALRA, 1989), the deliberations of 1993 Standing Advisory Commission on Human Rights (Lee, 1993), and the results of a series of surveys carried out in 1992, 1993 and 1994 by the Ulster Marketing Surveys Limited for the British Pregnancy Advisory Service. The latter demonstrated public opinion largely in favour of the liberalisation of abortion law in Northern Ireland.

A further focal point was Helen Axby's 1994 survey which showed an overwhelming majority of her sample in favour of extension of the 1967 British Abortion Act to Northern Ireland, a finding reiterated in this survey update. In 2001, the issue has been amplified once again following fpaNI's success in being granted leave for a judicial review of current abortion law in Northern Ireland to clarify what Professor Simon Lee (1995) has deemed a 'twilight zone'.[4]

---

[4] Ambiguities in the law make its interpretation difficult. Abortions are carried out for 'therapeutic reasons', generally regarded as being (i) the woman has a serious medical or psychological problem which would jeopardise her life or health if the pregnancy were to continue; (ii) the woman has severe learning difficulties, (iii) abnormality of the foetus is detected. However, doctors are given no clear guidelines, hence the low numbers of abortions performed.

Given this weight of evidence, two questions are asked repeatedly:- why it is that abortion is largely exported from one part of the UK to another, and why only 50-80 women each year can access abortion provision in Northern Ireland itself under a piece of Victorian legislation that remains unamended since 1945. The responses received from the NI women, all of whom so readily agreed to be involved in this survey, serve as testament to the call for normalisation through legal reform. Moreover, it is hoped that this report will act as a call to end the lonely journey so many have had to make over too many years.

The findings

Respondents' personal profile: age, education and employment

Age

The 1994 survey noted that 22% of its sample were teenagers and that the rest were equally divided between the age groups 20-24 (38%) and 25-40 (37%), while only one woman was identified as over forty.

The overall results of the 2000/1 survey indicate an increase amongst those aged 20 and under (33%). Those aged 21-24 accounted for 19%, the 25-29's for 25%, and the 30-39's 20%. Four were aged 40+.

While the 1994 survey sample was located entirely at MSI centres in Britain, the mix of respondents completing questionnaires at MSI in Britain (105) and fpaNI in Belfast (50) for the 2000/1 survey presented some interesting contrasts. One important example is the age differential highlighted in Table 1 when the sample is broken down according to source.

Table 1 – Age profile according to source (actual numbers surveyed in parentheses)

Age Category	20 and under	21-24	25-29	30-39	40+
MSI sample (105)	26% (27)	19% (20)	30% (32)	24% (25)	1% (1)
fpaNI sample (50)	50% (25)	18% (9)	14% (7)	12% (6)	6% (3)

Although all age categories are represented in both samples, the strong presence of women aged 25+ in the MSI sample may well be accounted for by their greater experience and confidence in using direct access routes, such as the Yellow Pages and the internet, thereby bypassing intermediaries.

Conversely, half of the women in the fpaNI sample are in the 20 or under age group. All of these have availed themselves of the counselling and referral services offered in Northern Ireland, which, given their immaturity, is a process likely to have been actively supported by their families, and in some cases by professionals.

Superficially, the combined sample figure of 33% (52 out of 155) of women aged 20 or under would seem to be at variance with official data where only 19% in 1998 and 20% in 2000 of NI women attending British abortion clinics are teenagers (Source: ONS). However, putting aside the fpaNI figure because of the special circumstances explained above, the figure of 26% for the MSI sample is not at variance with official figures when adjustment is made for the fact that these record teenagers only, while this survey recorded abortions for those aged 20 or under.

Education and Employment

Over half (57%) of those taking part in the 2000/1 survey remained in full-time education until the age of 18. The proportion was slightly less (53%) in the 1994 survey.

The numbers in employment amounted to 63%, 13% were unemployed and 24% indicated that they were full-time students. No questions relating to employment profile were asked in the 1994 survey.

On the basis of the educational levels attained by NI women in the 1994 survey, the inference drawn was that they were a predominantly middle class sample (Furedi, ed., 1995). While such an assumption could also be made about the sample in the 2000/1 survey, it must be pointed out that no question was posed, either in the 1994 or in the current survey, which would reveal the respondent's class, either by virtue of her education or occupation.

When considering the under 20s in the 2000/1 sample, a higher proportion is inevitably seen to be still in the education system (73%). Unemployment in this group is 10%. Even when the respondents are divided into MSI and fpaNI samples, there is little variation (see Table 2).

Table 2 – Educational and employment profile of women aged 20 and under (actual numbers surveyed in parentheses)

	Student	Employed	Unemployed
MSI sample (27)	67% (18)	22% (6)	11% (3)
fpaNI sample (25)	80% (20)	12% (3)	8% (2)
Total	73% (38)	17% (9)	10% (5)

Official statistics (NI Statistics & Research Agency, 2001) using the Labour Force Survey (LFS), record a 3% unemployment figure for women aged 16-59 and 4% for those aged between 16 and 34. This is a much smaller figure than that found in this survey (10%). However, the difference is best explained as a consequence of the strict definition of the unemployed in the official statistics, rather than a higher propensity for abortions among unemployed women.[5]

Irrespective of their level of education or their occupational status, interviews with younger women at MSI clinics brought to light a concern that parenthood should be an intentional choice. A strong desire was also expressed for a stable relationship and a sound economic environment in which to bring up children. They spoke of their hope of establishing themselves in jobs or careers amenable to a balance between family and working life. One in particular stands out:

> *I'm a single mother of two children and I'm just like all the girls in my area. All of them have wee ones. There's not much else to do. But I want better for myself and my kids. They are still small, but I want to do a course later on and get a job. My Mum wants me to get on, too, and she'll help me with the kids.*

---

[5] The International Labour Office (ILO) measure of unemployment used refers to people without a job who were available to start work the two weeks following their Labour Force Survey (LFS) interview and had either looked for work in the four weeks prior to interview, or were waiting to start a job they had already obtained.

A dramatic example of a young woman university student aged 19, who reluctantly opted for an abortion in the event of a crisis pregnancy, is given in the following interview extract:

> I belong to ...[a fundamentalist Christian church] and I believe that what I'm doing is wrong. I actually believe that I am going to commit murder today. But myself and my boyfriend have decided that this is not the right time to have a baby, as we are not even half way in our university courses.

Both of these young respondents remarked that they regretted having received little or no sex education or impartial advice on an unwanted pregnancy at school.[6]

Accessing the abortion

The process of accessing an abortion, from the time before the decision is made to arrival at the clinic (see Tables 3 to 7), has been probed in greater detail than in the 1994 survey. This has been done in order to highlight the number and the nature of the obstacles NI women have to confront. Also highlighted are difficulties encountered by non-NI women as a point of comparison.

Help with the decision

Table 3 – Who helped with decision? (actual numbers surveyed in parentheses)

GP	Counsellor	Partner	Family Member	Friend	No-one
5% (7)	6% (9)	32% (49)	8% (13)	15% (24)	45% (70)

Note: Multiple choices were allowed.

---

[6]Preliminary results from a survey, Towards Better Sexual Health being conducted jointly by fpaNI and the University of Ulster found that half the young people surveyed had intercourse between the ages of 10 and 15, and more than a third did not use a condom (Irish News, 31 July 2001). Unplanned teenage pregnancy and parenthood is also the subject of a consultative document published by the Department of Health, Social Services and Public Safety (2000). The NI Department of Education is expected to introduce the new Relationships and Sexuality Education (RSE) guidelines in the 2001 academic year.

Of those who gave a positive response, a significant number stated they had discussed the decision with their partners. In comparing Axby's 1994 sample where 25% had discussed their abortion decision with a partner, Boyle (1997) contrasts this unfavourably with an 85% sample of US women who declared they had involved their partners (Major et al, 1990). The current figure, although not reaching the level of the US study, indicates a progressive trend.

When asked about other women's abortions, those indicating no such knowledge remains fairly constant (roughly one in three in both surveys). However, a considerable proportion then and now knew of two, three, and up to twelve women (an overall average of almost 2).

Table 4 – How many NI women do you know who have had an abortion? (actual numbers surveyed in parentheses)

No. known	0	1	2	3	4	5	6	7-12
Respondents	32% (50)	21% (32)	17% (26)	12% (19)	9% (14)	4% (7)	2% (3)	3% (4)

No question linking this knowledge and an individual respondent's decision was asked in the questionnaire. However, in interview many cited the intensive discussions they had with friends, and sometimes sisters, as crucial, in the absence of public information.

In the case of the 30 non-NI interviewees, a similar pattern emerged, with the majority having discussed their pregnancy and abortion decision with their partner, and sometimes with selected friends and family members. There were some, however, who were very keen for total, or almost total secrecy to be maintained, and these included women of English origin.

Sources of information on the clinic

Amongst the fpaNI sample, 78% were provided with information on the clinic by the organisation itself. The MSI sample, in contrast, shows a much greater diversity in sources (see Table 5). What is common to both samples is the scant evidence of GPs being cited as a source of information about the clinic.

Table 5 – Where did you get information on the clinic? (actual numbers surveyed in parentheses)

	fpaNI sample (50)	MSI sample (105)
GP	2% (1)	11% (12)
FPA	78% (39)	0
Friend	0	22% (23)
Relative	6% (3)	6% (6)
Advertisement	0	5% (5)
Magazine	0	9% (9)
Yellow Pages	14% (7)	35% (37)
Internet	0	9% (10)
Women's centres	0	3% (3)

The role of GPs

Interviews revealed confusion amongst GPs about abortion provisions in Northern Ireland. The most extreme example was of a mother of three, with one child suffering from a severely debilitating disease, and another with a Special Needs syndrome. Her comment on her GP was as follows:

> *I went to my GP thinking I would get every bit of support I needed in getting referred for an abortion. After all, the GP knew of my situation and the terrible strain I am under as a result of my marriage being on the rocks. I've had lots of treatment for my nerves. But I couldn't believe his attitude. He just sat there as cool as a breeze and said he understood my predicament but that the law tied his hand. He didn't even suggest a test for foetal abnormality. I was so angry I just went straight down to Dublin with the kids to see my sister. It was her doctor who sorted me out, gave me all the information I needed. But I still ended up paying out a small fortune. If anyone is*

*entitled to a free abortion, it's me. And I am supposed
to be a British citizen...*

Of the 53 women in the combined samples who consulted their
GPs, 31 stated they received all relevant information about possible
choices, 15 stated the GP was unsupportive and 7 said an attempt
was made to dissuade them from having an abortion.

The figure of 31 (53%) women receiving relevant information on
possible choices corroborates the findings of MSI's (1999) study of
GPs where almost 46% of Northern Ireland GPs indicated a
broadly pro-choice position versus 82% of GPs in the UK overall.
However, when it came to actual referrals, GPs rarely featured (see
Table 6). The figure for GP referrals in the 1994 survey was 17%.

*Table 6 – Who made the referral? (actual numbers surveyed in
parentheses)*

	GP	fpaNI	Self
MSI sample (105)	7% (7)	5% (5)	88% (93)
fpaNI sample (50)	0	100% (50)	0

The considerable number of self-referrals in the MSI sample has
already been related to the abilities and the sophistication of this
group in accessing public information pathways. In interview, some
expressed a preference for bypassing counselling and referral
services in Northern Ireland.

Several amongst the self-referrals stated they did not wish a
counsellor to take them through the various options open to them,
even at the clinic. The very act of having travelled to Britain should
be sufficient proof of their decision, they insisted. This was a factor
amongst Irish women also noted by O'Hare (1997) during her
seven years as an abortion counsellor in Britain, and by Mahon,
Conlon and Dillon (1998) in their study of women from the
Republic of Ireland at British clinics commissioned by the
government of the Irish Republic.

A fairly commonly repeated quip by NI interviewees was that they
preferred to give their GP 'a wide berth', even at the pregnancy
testing stage. One teenager said:

> *I would never advise anyone to go to a GP, whatever he or she thinks about abortion. My test result was clearly written up in my notes and was seen by the surgery reception staff. The news was all round [the small, rural town] by lunchtime and people started asking me how I was feeling and did I have morning sickness yet? I will have to put it about that I had a miscarriage when I go back.*

Non-NI interviewees painted a picture of the difficulties they also experienced with their GPs. In Britain, GPs who have a conscientious objection to abortion have an obligation under their terms of service to refer a patient to another doctor as soon as possible. However, anecdotal evidence of the type provided by non-NI interviewees indicate that conscientious objectors in the medical profession, allowed for under the 1967 Act, do not necessarily observe their obligation. Access to an NHS-funded abortion, whether in a hospital or in a dedicated private sector clinic,[7] can be affected, not only by GP attitude, but also by the level of funding provided by the Health Authority.[8]

In the sample of 30 non-NI respondents, 7 stated that they found their GPs supportive, had all possible choices discussed with them, and when opting for an abortion, received a referral letter for an NHS-funded termination. However, 2 stated their GPs were extremely unhelpful, but finally gave referral letters. The Brook Advisory Service was involved in NHS referrals in a further 3 cases.

Of the 11 non-NI women who paid for their abortions, 6 said that their GPs were either unsympathetic to their situation or declared that they were totally opposed to abortion. A woman suffering from a sexually transmitted infection who had become pregnant, despite being on the contraceptive pill, said:

> *My female GP gave me short shrift. She just gave me a leaflet and little or no time. She should have discussed my situation with me, as I found out later that the*

---

[7] A study found that 45,000 abortions are funded by the NHS in the private sector. Of these 85% are provided by two charities – Marie Stopes International and the British Pregnancy Advisory Service (Abortion Law Reform Association, 2000).

[8] An Abortion Law Reform Association survey of Health Authorities in 1999 found that the national average in 1999 was 74% of abortions funded. It also found that several Health Authorities set specific criteria for approval and even where this does not occur, there is often restriction by waiting time. This means that women often opt to fund the abortion themselves.

*medication I was on could have damaged the foetus. I
felt I was being judged by her. The clinic was fine and
gave me all the information I needed. I opted to pay.*

Some, when confronted by a long delay (11 weeks in one case),
decided to refer themselves and pay, rather than wait. Others, and
these included women of Asian origin, wished to bypass their GP
entirely. A university student in her final year, explained:

*Our GP is an Indian and a family friend. If my
parents fond out life would become a nightmare for
me. It's not that my family is against abortion.
Actually, if they knew about my situation they would
insist on an abortion anyway. What they are against is
sex outside of marriage and in their eyes I have
become 'soiled'. Even though I was born here, they
still expect to have some say in choosing my marriage
partner. You know, they would insist on me marrying
someone of our caste and religion. I am a Hindu and
my boyfriend is a Muslim. That's dynamite – there's
nothing worse in our culture.*

Raising money for the abortion

Raising money for a private abortion was an ordeal for many of the
women concerned. The sources given by NI women in Table 7 below
corresponded to those non-Irish women gave, although several
students amongst the latter group said they had extended their
student loans to meet costs. Nearly all non-NI interviewees lived in
the Greater London area, and consequently, the journey to the clinic
and travel expenses were not a particular burden. Proximity to the
clinic also meant that the woman was frequently accompanied by at
least one person to support her.

*Table 7 – How money was raised. Combined samples (155) (actual
numbers surveyed in parentheses)*

Partner	20% (31)
Family	20% (32)
Friends	2% (4)
Self	37% (57)
Multiple Sources	20% (31)

Note: (a) Borrowing occurred in 43% of instances; (b) multiple choices
were allowed.

The journey to the clinic

Although no questions on the journey itself were asked in the questionnaire, the logistics of travel, and its emotional and financial costs were explored in some detail in the interviews. This aspect was invariably cited by NI women as a major source of stress, sometimes worse than the abortion itself.

The principal financial outlay was the abortion procedure which ranged, depending on the stage of pregnancy, from £380 to £615 at MSI London centres. Regardless of whether women chose to have a local or a general anaesthetic, the termination was conducted on the basis of daycare, ostensibly removing the need to find overnight accommodation. The introduction of daycare for NI women and those from the Republic results from the recent removal of the Department of Health's residency requirement following the abortion.[9]

Despite the removal of the residency requirement, some women reported difficulties in being able to return home on the same day, thus adding between £25 and £50 to their expenditure for overnight accommodation. These difficulties ranged from inability to afford the very high cost charged by some airlines for day return flights, to being unable to make public transport connections late at night within Northern Ireland. This applied to women living in the rural areas (41%), some of whom did not have access to cars.

Furthermore, if women chose to have their abortions at the weekend, many found that some airlines impose a Saturday night stay-over, or in the case of some low-cost airlines, do not run a return flight on Saturdays. Interviewees reported that they had often invested a great deal of time and energy in contacting travel agents and airlines, only to find that the availability of cheap flights on any type of airline is something of a lottery, dependent on either early booking or last-minute luck. Costs of travel to respondents ranged from less than £100 to over £300.

Finding the money to cover expensive air travel often proved to be the straw that almost broke the camel's back. Women frequently wrote on their questionnaires that lack of funds meant that their abortion was delayed. Figures released by the ONS in 1999 show that 42% of women from England and Wales accessed their

---

[9]Under the Required Standard Operating Principles introduced in 2001

abortions in the first nine weeks of pregnancy, compared to only 32% of women from Northern Ireland. Rather than risk a delay, one woman wrote on her questionnaire:

> *I have been travelling all day and night. The only available flight had seats for £276 each, which is impossible to afford for myself and my mother. So we had to get a ferry to Stranraer in Scotland. Then we had to sit on the bus for 10 and-a-half hours. Getting into London at 6 a.m. it was still dark and I had no sleep. I am dreading the return journey this evening.*

Many of the interviewees remarked on the high cost of public transport to, and within London, especially if they had used airlines flying to destinations such as Luton and Stanstead. Those who were unused to foreign travel had little appreciation of the complexities involved in using unfamiliar transport systems. One said:

> *I was completely taken up with making the arrangements for the clinic appointment, sorting out a suitable flight, making sure the kids were being taken care of, and getting out of the house at the crack of the dawn without anyone knowing my business. I never gave a thought to the journey on the other side. The flight was late arriving in Stanstead, and then there was a train and a tube journey into West London which left me confused and exhausted. I had never been in London before. I didn't know how to use ticket machines with all this stuff about different zones. I tried to ask at the ticket desk, but the queue was a mile long, full of strangers like myself. Then I just stood there looking at people sailing through the automatic barrier. I thought I would get sliced in two. It all took so much time and I was petrified that I would miss my appointment. Luckily, in all that fuss and bother I remembered to phone the clinic to say I would be late.*

This interviewee spoke for many when she wryly remarked:

> *When I saw the clinic staff and all these English women in the waiting room looking so cool and collected, I said to myself, "They must think us Irish*

are a bag of nerves." But I bet they hadn't had the journey from hell. And then I had to face the same going back that night. It's just not fair.

Knowledge of organisations, such as the Irish Abortion Support Group in London, Escort in Liverpool, and of Women's Centres within Northern Ireland itself, as an additional strand of detailed local information and support, was limited. Twenty-four women stated they knew of the Women's Centres, but only 5 knew of services in England. It could well be deduced that 'alternative' sources are no longer so crucial as they once were, and that abortion has become much more 'mainstreamed'. Another factor is that access to daycare means that overnight accommodation, frequently provided by support groups in cases of financial need in the past, is now less in demand.

Views on legislative change

Table 8 – Legislative change and abortion provision in NI. Combined samples (155) (actual numbers surveyed in parentheses)

	Yes	No	Undecided
In favour of extension of 1967 abortion act	95% (148)	1% (2)	3% (5)
Preference for abortion in NI	95% (148)	4% (7)	0

The overwhelming majority of respondents (95% in 2000/1, 96% in 1994) who stated that they wished for a change in the law is matched by the similar numbers (95% in 2000/1, 91% in 1994) who indicated they would prefer to have their abortions in Northern Ireland. Although not posed in the questionnaire, the question of NHS-funded abortions in Britain for Northern Irish women was asked in the interviews. All but two women out of thirty strongly agreed that such provision should be made available in the period between now and progressive legislative change in Northern Ireland.

Discussion

Comparing the 1994 and 2000/2001 surveys

Broadly speaking, the current results concur with those of the 1994 survey. The difficulties reported then by NI women in accessing information, the referral process, and the abortion itself, are as true now as they were then. Despite the increasing numbers of women who have had abortions (at least 40,000 over the past 20 years), inevitably resulting in knowledge being spread by word of mouth, access to detailed information is still a problem. Apart from some GPs, only the fpaNI at its two centres offers an abortion counselling and referral service across the whole of Northern Ireland. The ordeal of raising money in a short timespan has remained unchanged.

Comparing NI and non-NI respondents

Given that all non-NI respondents lived within the Greater London area, thus encountering no travel difficulties, the journey to the clinic proved to be the main point of contrast between the two groups. However, as pointed up in the main body of the report, some non-NI women experienced problems which mirrored those of NI women, in particular, difficulties with GPs, failure to access an NHS-funded termination and trouble in raising funds.

Similarities between both sets of women also extended beyond these areas. One of these, the stress on maintaining secrecy about the abortion beyond a small, intimate circle, was expressed by both groups, although this was more extreme in the case of NI women. NI respondents reported they engaged in elaborate forms of subterfuge to conceal the nature of their journey, such as shopping trips to London or visits to friends 'down the country'. This often involved making purchases which they could ill afford, something which one respondent said felt like a 'last desperate spree of a gambler when she's on her uppers'.

Non-NI women disclosed more minor 'white lies', in particular to employers who would not categorise abortion as a health issue. Attitudes of employers to time off from work in this context must be a matter of concern to trades unions, health and women's groups on both sides of the Irish Sea.

Silence, or worse, demonisation of abortion in the public arena in Northern Ireland adds to the pressure to maintain secrecy. Boyle and McEvoy (1998) in their study of seven NI abortion- seekers point out the key role religion plays in this. Their interviewees talked of the 'strongly negative construction of abortion being "hammered" and "pounded" into them, being "rammed" down their throats', an ordeal also undergone by respondents in this survey. For women in Northern Ireland motherhood is a powerful signifier, reinforced by the predominantly denominational nature of the education system.

The centrality of religion in shoring up a sense of difference between Protestant and Catholic has been a source of tension since the creation of the Northern Ireland state in 1921, following the partitioning of the island. Rolston and Eggert (1994) point to the paradox of both religions' intense focus on moral issues, particularly on sexuality, which has proved to be a singular source of unity across 'the divide'. The claim made by a Northern Irish politician to substantiate this phenomenon: 'We might have been fighting and killing ourselves for years but we are united when it comes to opposing abortion' (Simpson, 1996), is frequently quoted.

In recent times, however, such public unity is fraying at the edges despite the rejection by a majority vote at the NI Assembly of extension of the 1967 British Abortion Act in June, 2000[10]. Three political parties with representation in the NI Assembly have adopted a pro-choice policy and are in favour of extension of the 1967 Act – the Women's Coalition, the Progressive Unionist Party (PUP) and the Ulster Democratic Party (UDP). Two other parties represented at the Assembly, the Alliance Party and the Ulster Unionist Party, led by David Trimble, have no official party line on abortion and treat the issue as a matter of personal conscience. Amongst others represented at the Assembly, the Social and Democratic Labour Party (SDLP) is opposed, and the Democratic Unionist Party (DUP), led by Ian Paisley, allows for abortion only where the pregnant woman's life is in danger. Sinn Fein is also opposed, except where the woman's life or mental health is in grave danger, and in the case of rape or sexual abuse. This position appears to be broadly in line with the existing legislation dating to 1861.

Against the continuingly difficult, but changing attitudes to abortion in Northern Ireland, women tread their way through a

---

[10]Matters concerning criminal law, which includes abortion, still fall within the remit of the British parliament, rather than the NI Assembly.

minefield of virulent anti-choice rhetoric in the public arena and their own inner conflicts in the private one. In this context, the complexities surrounding the keeping and breaking of silence can be understood. As researchers (Fletcher, 1995, Boyle and McEvoy, 1998) indicate, a distinction needs to be made between public and private spheres. In the public sphere, there is fear of exposure, not only of one's self, but also of family in an environment of political, anti-abortion rhetoric and criminalisation. In such conditions women are required to bear what one writer describes as a 'personal burden of shame for a society in denial' (de Burgh, 2000).

In contrast, the private sphere may well contain friends and family members who are pro-choice, and, as can be seen from statistical evidence presented in this survey, may themselves have had experience of abortion. Given the number of NI respondents in this survey who declared themselves in favour of progressive abortion legislation (95%), individuals – partner, family member(s), friend(s) – they stated knew of their abortion, and their own knowledge of other women's, the issue of silence and secrecy, so much associated with NI women, and Irish women generally, needs to be re-evaluated.

Even in Britain, where abortion has been legalised since 1968, Neustatter (1986) remarks on the paradox of abortion's high public profile and its position as a shameful secret in many British women's lives. Hadley (1996) confirms this when she notes that abortion features regularly in the media and is a 'stock element in the roundabout of soap opera crises – will she, won't she? Brookside, EastEnders, Coronation Street, even The Archers...Yet [it] is still not talked about much in everyday conversation. Few women admit to having had one without being sure they are among friends. It is too personal, it is still taboo.'

More recently, Zoe Williams (2000), writing in the London Evening Standard, argues, '...abortion is the only taboo we have left. Like non-prescription drugs, and homosexuality, and everything else which once was unthinkable and isn't anymore, abortion is always going to spark a debate of some sort...' Another journalist, Nicci Gerrard (2001), asks in her Observer article why it is that, 'One in three women has had an abortion[11] and 92 per cent of us agree with the right to choose. So why are we still ashamed to talk about its effect on our lives?'

---

[11]The 1999 figures for England and Wales are 183,250 (Source: Office of Population Censuses and Surveys).

In the light of these observations, it would seem important to avoid pathologising Irish women's failure to engage in public discourse by an over-emphasis of their exceptionalism.

For far too long, Irish women have been consigned to an 'abortion ghetto' where they are perceived, especially by the British media, and sometimes by their Irish counterparts, as haunted by moral guilt and irrationally obsessed by the fear of being 'found out'. While this stereotype may have resonance in some instances, it hardly accounts for those – and they are not a mere few – who are distressed by the whole abortion-seeking experience, but are not traumatised. It does not account for the women in this study who stated that while being comfortable with their abortion choice, they were not willing to be publicly vilified and even persecuted for making that choice.

It is ironic that the personal stories of the Irish and non-NI respondents mirrored each other in many respects. Listening to their testimonies, and overhearing the strained conversations of women from Britain at the clinics, as well as exchanges in French, German, Portuguese and Spanish between women forced to abort in Britain due to the limitations of their countries' abortion laws, only served to reinforce their commonality. Clearly, all had experienced different, but always difficult journeys, emotional and otherwise.

Recommendations

Extension of the British 1967 Abortion Act to Northern Ireland as a prelude to the introduction of more progressive legislation.

Funding of NI women's abortions at British clinics as an interim step.

GP training, pre and post-registration, on abortion law in Northern Ireland and in Britain. Training to include all aspects of accessing an abortion.

GPs holding a conscientious objection to abortion to be obliged to declare it to their patients. Further, that they be required to refer to a pro-choice doctor.

Training for support staff to be introduced on the need for confidentiality, especially for those in GP surgeries.

Sex education in schools to have clear guidelines on the choices available in an unplanned pregnancy, including abortion.

School nurses to receive training on guidelines on the full range of choices available in an unplanned pregnancy, and on imparting these to students in a balanced way.

Acknowledgements

We would like to thank the following: Helen Axby, Tony Kerridge and Liz Davies of Marie Stopes International (MSI) for making the survey possible; the MSI centre staff who bore our intrusions stoically; Audrey Simpson and the counselling staff at fpaNI who ensured that 50 of the questionnaires were completed, and who advised and helped us at crucial stages; members and supporters of the Irish Abortion Solidarity Campaign (Iasc) for being so generous help with the research; Clare O'Hagan for donating the artwork for the cover; the Irish Women's Abortion Support Group (IWASG) and the Simon Population Fund for a financial contribution; the membership of the Voice for Choice Campaign who supported the project; Dr. Rayah Feldman of the University of the South Bank, London, for her helpful comments on the text, and Dr. Gautam Appa of the London School of Economics for providing extensive support on the analysis of the statistics. Above all, we would like to express our gratitude to the 185 women who participated in the survey and gave it their warm support. They did so in the hope that in the not too distant future Northern Irish women will be treated with dignity and care in their own place.

References

Abortion Law Reform Association (ALRA), no date, Improving Access to Abortion: A guide, London.

Axby, H. (1994) Client Survey: Women Attending From Northern Ireland, London, Marie Stopes International UK Clinics.

Boyle, M. (1997) Re-Thinking Abortion, Psychology, gender, power and the law, London, Routledge.

Boyle, M. and McEvoy, J. (1998) 'Putting abortion in its social context: Northern Irish women's experiences of abortion in England', Health, Vol.2, No.3: 283-304.

Buckley, M (1997) 'Sitting on Your Politics: The Irish Among the British and the Women Among in the Irish' in J. Mac Laughlin (ed), Location and Dislocation in Contemporary Irish Society, Emigration and Irish Identities, Cork, Cork University Press.

de Burgh, S. (2000), 'Preface', The Irish Journey, Women's Stories of Abortion, Dublin, Irish Family Planning Association.

Department of Health, Social Services and Public Safety (2000), Myths & Reality, Teenage Pregnancy and Parenthood, Consultative Document, Belfast.

Family Planning Association Northern Ireland (fpaNI) (2001) Challenge, Issue 1, May.

Fletcher, R. (1995) 'Silences: Irish Women and Abortion', Feminist Review, 50: 44-66.

Furedi, A. (ed.) (1995) The Abortion Law in Northern Ireland: Human rights and reproductive choice, Belfast, Family Planning Association Northern Ireland.

Gerrard, N. (2001) 'Damned if you do...'. Observer, 22 April.

Hadley, J. (1996) Abortion: Between Freedom and Necessity, London, Virago.

Lee, S. (1993) Abortion in Northern Ireland: The Report of an International Tribunal, Belfast.

Lee, S. (1995) 'Abortion law in Northern Ireland: the twilight zone' in A. Furedi (ed.) (1995) ibid.

Levine, J. (1982) Sisters. The Personal Story of an Irish Feminist, Swords, Ward River Press.

Marie Stopes International (MSI) (1999) General Practitioners: attitudes to abortion, A Report, London.

Mahon, M., Conlon, C. & Dillon, L. (1998) Women and Crisis Pregnancy, Dublin, Government Publications Office.

Major, B., Cozzarelli, C., Sciacchitano., A.M., Cooper, M.L., Testa, M. and Mueller, P.M. (1990) 'Perceived social support, self-efficacy and adjustment to abortion', Journal of Personality and Social Psychology 59: 452-63.

Neustatter, A. with Newson, G. (1986) Mixed Feelings: The Experience of Abortion, London, Pluto Press.

Northern Ireland Abortion Law Reform Association (NIALRA) (1989), Abortion in Northern Ireland, the Report of an International Tribunal, Belfast, Beyond the Pale Publications.

Northern Ireland Statistics and Research Agency (2001) Women in Northern Ireland, July 2001.

O'Hare, P. (1997) 'Abortion Seeking Women from Ireland – What are their Counselling Needs?' in E. Lee and M. Lattimer (eds.),

Issues in Pregnancy Counselling: What Do Women Need and Want?, Canterbury, Pro-Choice Forum.

Rolston, B. and Eggert, A. (1994) 'Ireland' in A. Eggert and B. Rolston (eds.), Abortion in the New Europe, London, Greenwood.

Ruane, M. (2000), 'Introduction', The Irish Journey, ibid.

Simpson, A. (1996) Abortion and Northern Ireland. Paper presented at a conference entitled 'Abortion Law in Britain: What do Women Want?', New College Oxford, November.

Williams, Z. (2000) 'Is Abortion the Last Taboo?', London Evening Standard, 3 March.

SUBJECT INDEX